Technical Foundations of Client/Server Systems

Technical Foundations of Client/Server Systems

Carl L. Hall

A Wiley–QED Publication

John Wiley & Sons, Inc.

New York • Chichester • Brisbane • Toronto • Singapore

Publisher: Katherine Schowalter
Editor: Ed Kerr
Managing Editor: Angela Murphy
Editorial Production & Design: Publishers' Design and Production Services

Designations used by companies to distinguish their products are often claimed as trademarks. In all instances where John Wiley & Sons, Inc. is aware of a claim, the product names appear in initial capital or all capital letters. Readers, however, should contact the appropriate companies for more complete information regarding trademarks and registration.

This text is printed on acid-free paper.

Library of Congress Cataloging-in-Publication Data

Hall, Carl.
　　Technical foundations of client/server systems / Carl Hall.
　　　　p.　　cm.
　　"A Wiley/QED publication."
　　Includes index.
　　ISBN 0-471-06086-0 (alk. paper)
　　1. Client/server computing.　I. Title.
QA76.9.C55H34　1994
004'.36—dc20　　　　　　　　　　　　　　　　94-20180

Printed in the United States of America
10 9 8 7 6 5 4 3 2 1

Contents

Preface

Client/server technology is the technology of the 1990s. As the need for greater flexibility, more computing power, and the empowerment of employees is recognized, client/server technology and its extensions into distributed and cooperative computing is becoming accepted as the basis for building the future.

Use this book as the title indicates, to build a basic foundation of knowledge about client/server. Developing specifications for client/server platforms that will deliver proper capabilities to a given enterprise is not always a simple task. This book provides the information necessary for asking the correct questions and evaluating answers. In a sense, this book can provide ammunition to protect you against overblown claims by vendors. Use it that way.

Anyone with a background in computing who desires to understand the basic principles underlying this new, popular method of computing should read this book. It will be especially useful to Chief Information Officers, Information Systems managers, Application programmers and System programmers. Network administrators and architects will also find the book useful as an introduction to the technology that will affect their careers throughout the 1990s and beyond. Database administrators and knowledge engineers should be aware of the information in this book so that they can take advantage of new technology as it becomes available.

In spite of widespread acceptance, client/server technology is not completely understood by many IS professionals. Trade publications and current books create a confusing picture of what it is all about. There are even a few people who think installing a database server is the final step to take to arrive at client/server benefits. The discussion on Enhanced Client/Server functionality will expose capabilities and power that may surprise many people.

The owner of the small company and the senior executive of the large company must each gain some knowledge of what can be done and how it can benefit their particular bottom line. Then, each must find the proper people who can do the technical things that will bring the magic to their own organization.

This book provides an introduction to current client/server technology. It includes information on the three most common types of client/server paradigms: file servers, database servers, and Enhanced Client/Server capabilities supported by new open operating systems and transaction processing systems. Information is included about extensions into the world of distributed and cooperative processing and how these systems can be used to provide the computing tools necessary for the success of the modern enterprise.

Many people have been disappointed with their implementation of client/server because of poor performance, higher-than-expected cost, or both. Reading the chapters on database servers and Enhanced Client/Server will provide information about how to correct these problems, or how to prevent problems if the enterprise is just deciding how to implement this exciting new paradigm.

The book is written in such a way that it will appeal to anyone involved with information systems. Most sections can be understood without knowledge of programming or advanced technical issues. A few chapters dig a little deeper and require at least a reading knowledge of C, but even these chapters can be generally understood by anyone who is basically computer literate.

The intent of this book is to define and explain the principles of client/server. Some subjects are described in more detail than others in order to provide the level of understanding required to properly evaluate and choose client/server products. To some, the level of detail will seem uneven. To others, more detail would be very helpful. The reader should consult the bibliography for sources of more information.

The development of client/server technology begins with an overview, and builds in each chapter from the simplest aspect of the technology, the file server, through to the concepts of Enhanced Client/Server.

The chapter on Enhanced Client/Server technology will be very important to anyone planning a system where the data is distributed among multiple servers. The use of Enhanced Client/Server becomes nearly the only economical method when using a Wide Area Network (WAN) because the cost of providing sufficient network capacity (bandwidth) to accommodate database calls is so high. If there will be more than one type of database (heterogeneous databases) in the system and/or data tables will be distributed, it becomes absolutely necessary to use Enhanced Client/Server systems.

The discussion of Enhanced Client/Server Processing uses TUXEDO System/T from UNIX System Laboratories as an example of the technology available. It includes examples of using System/T to illustrate how this technology is best used.

A complete client/server system must include the capability to manage both the stored information and the application programs that interpret and manipulate that information. In any complex or large system, only a fully developed Transaction Processing system can deliver all required capabilities. In their book, *Transaction Processing: Concepts and Techniques*, Jim Gray and Andreas Reuter state that "In a nutshell: without transactions, distributed systems cannot be made to work for typical real-live applications."

The following quote is from the *Oracle Integrator*, Volume 3, Number 6, December 1992, in the article "Distributed Computing Architectures for the 90s."

> In an environment where a single table will be distributed across multiple systems, it is desirable to route inserts that are entered into any one system to a specific system based on a data values in the row to be inserted.

The software products needed to support this architecture are just beginning to appear on the market. A good example is support for X/Open's XA interface, an often overlooked feature in Oracle7. The XA interface is an industry standard means for integrating two-phase commit database managers, such as Oracle7, with a distributed transaction processing (DTP) manager such as Transarc's Encina, UNIX International's TUXEDO* and NCR's Top End. These DTP managers provide the capability to interconnect multiple, heterogeneous hardware platforms, operating systems, and databases as currently exist in many Fortune 500 corporations and federal agencies.

Because transaction processing is so central to successful client/server operation, there is considerable emphasis placed on explaining how transaction process works and why it is necessary.

The example systems in this book are intended to illustrate how to design and develop systems using the principles described. They are incomplete because of space limitations. Hopefully, they are sufficiently complete to aid the reader in applying the principles learned.

Network calculations are likewise incomplete and are rather simplistic (for instance, they do not include the load of network protocol data), since they are intended only to illustrate the points made. In a real situation, network calculations must include full consideration of protocol data, address collisions on some networks, and other network overhead items.

Certain products have been described in more detail and used in the example applications. This use in no way implies any endorsement of these products. They were chosen as representative of their genre. All products mentioned in this book are excellent and can be used within the limits of their capabilities very effectively. Also, no implication should be drawn about a product that was not mentioned. The purpose of this book is to provide information of a general nature and cites products only as examples.

---

*Actually, Novell's UNIX System Laboratories is the vendor of TUXEDO. TUXEDO is endorsed by UNIX International.

It is not intended to be a catalog, so many fine products have not been mentioned.

Open systems are becoming increasingly popular, especially to support client/server. There is no direct discussion of open systems here, but many of the discussions that you will encounter are predicated on open systems principles. Those planning client/server installations should carefully consider using a system that is compliant with open systems standards, such as POSIX and X/Open specifications.

Open systems and UNIX are often equated, and for good reason. UNIX is the basis of operating systems standards which have been developed and which will be developed, but UNIX is not the only open system available. Even most proprietary systems have a high level of openness. What makes UNIX, and its derivatives, truly open is that they are available on almost any hardware. Applications developed for a UNIX platform can be relatively easily moved to any other UNIX platform. (Notice that the porting is not entirely free; some modifications are almost always required.)

Another fact about the UNIX-type systems is that there are a large number of system tools available. Those who have used UNIX for a considerable time, and then have again worked with an older proprietary system soon miss the variety of tools from UNIX. And more are on the way.

More open systems can be expected in the future. The existence of standards such as POSIX and specifications such as XPG3 from X/Open provide a basis that allows vendors to develop new systems that differ greatly internally but remain open for use because they are compliant with these standards.

Information on related subjects such as standards, two-phase commit, and a glossary are provided in Appendixes and, although they are very useful, they are not reading that is required to understand the rest of the book.

TRADEMARKS

OS/2, RS/6000, IMS, IMS/DC are trademarks or registered trademarks of International Business Machines Corporation.

1

Introduction

1.1 OVERVIEW

Client/server technology is a paradigm made possible by a combination of powerful computer hardware and reliable, fast, and relatively low-cost communication technology. A number of concepts, including distributed computing, cooperative computing, and distributed transaction processing, are associated with client/server technology. Client/server systems have moved computing from a single, monolithic, centrally administered system to a distributed system providing fast, economical access to information for everyone.

The monolithic system, shown in Figure 1.1, is a logical representation of the mainframe approach. The "One Big Computer" may actually be several central processors made into a logical single unit by hardware and software.

Figure 1.2 illustrates how Client/Server technology can be used to empower people. Each branch office has a local computer with necessary data, while the home office maintains central files on a larger set of servers. A properly designed C/S system can support thousands of users with high performance.

Client/server technology has become popular because the technology:

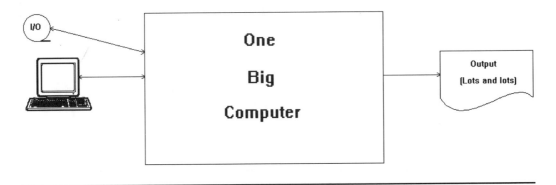

Figure 1.1   The monolithic system.

- Allows use of lower-cost hardware.
- Supports scalability.
- Supports better fault-tolerant systems.
- Provides easier management of distributed data.
- Supports Graphical User Interface (GUI) front ends that make user interfaces better and smarter.

1.2   SOME BASIC CLIENT/SERVER DEFINITIONS

One serious problem that people have with modern computing is that terms are not always defined and used in the same manner. Not only are there multiple meanings in use, but many people are not aware of this inexactness, resulting in confusion for the uninitiated. The use of ambiguous terms becomes even worse with client/server technology. Even the designation "client/server" has several meanings. The terms "distributed computing", "cooperative computing" and "distributed transaction processing" are used with even less accuracy. This section defines these and other terms exactly. See the glossary for additional definitions.

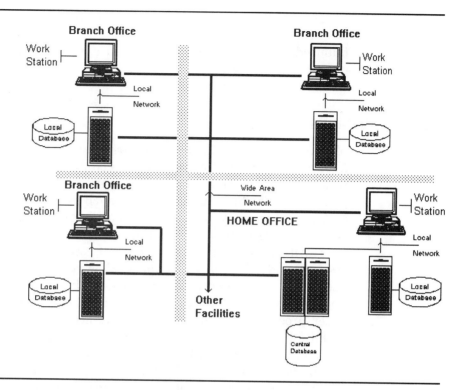

Figure 1.2   Using client/server in the enterprise.

1.2.1 Distributed Computing

The meaning of the term *distributed computing* is often taken for granted, yet it has different meanings to many different people. Generally, it refers to the case where more than one independent computer process is used to complete a specified task. The processes used may be on the same or different computing platforms. This definition is not very restrictive because it allows a multiple-step batch job to be included as a distributed computing system. Intuition says this is not right. Those who think in terms of batch can replace the word "task" with "job step," and the result will not be far from the correct definition.

Defining distributed computing in this way allows the term to encompass many computing paradigms, including C/S, distributed processing, and distributed databases. This book will use more exact terms, such as distributed processing and distributed database, for clarity.

1.2.2 Distributed Processing

M. Tamer Ozsu and Patrick Valduriez have called "the term *distributed processing* (or *distributed computing*) . . . probably the most abused term in computer science of the last couple of years . . . This abuse has gone on to such an extent that the term distributed processing has sometimes been called "a concept in search of a definition and a name.' "*

I will skip the controversy and not consider "distributed processing" and "distributed computing" as synonymous. Rather, as used here, distributed processing means that the processing of an application unit of work uses more than one independent computer process, the processes included are application processes and are not part of an operating system, database, or other support system. Thus distributed processing is defined as application capability, since any distribution of support processes (including database processing) is not apparent to the application developer. Only when the processing of an application can be distributed can the system be scalable and allow for use of multiple computer platforms by the application.

Distributed processing does not occur because various "job steps" may be done by different processes, as is done on mainframes. It is distributed processing only if a single unit of work is being done by multiple computer processes.

A distributed processing application may use the various processes in parallel or serially, depending on the application requirements. Further, these processes may be on different computer platforms, but processing on different platforms is not required to consider the application distributed.

Figure 1.3 illustrates distributed processing. A single appli-

---

*Ozsu, M. Tamer, and Patrick Valduriez, *Principles of Distributed Database Systems.* Englewood Cliffs, NJ: Prentice-Hall, Inc., 1991.

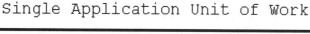

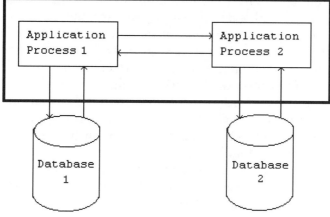

Figure 1.3   Distributed processing.

cation unit of work uses more than one process (in this case, two). The processes cooperate to complete the task by means of a communication protocol. Each application process may access a database independent of the other. The two databases may or may not be of the same type.

1.2.3 Distributed Database

A *database* can be defined as a collection of information permanently stored in a computer and accessible by a computer application to support application processing. This general definition has been made more specific by the use of specialized software, called database management systems (DBMS), and the more modern relational database management system (RDBMS).

In a *distributed database,* the data is divided among more than one database instance but may be treated as a single logical database by applications. A distributed database can exist on the same platform or, more usually, on multiple platforms. The concept of a distributed database is essential to an understanding of the implications of transaction management.

Most DBMSs provide for defining multiple instances of the database management software. In this case, each instance is called a database. These systems often also allow the definition of multiple *spaces,* which define the physical location of the data. When multiple spaces are defined for the same database, the DBMS manages the spaces as if they were logically one space (*spanning* the spaces), and the database is not considered distributed.

The concepts of distributed database and distributed processing are very different. A distributed database spreads the *data* into various locations. Distributed processing spreads the *processing* of the business application into various locations.

Figure 1.4 illustrates a distributed database. The application process communicates with the DBMS as if the database was at a single location. The DBMS manages the distribution of the data over multiple locations.

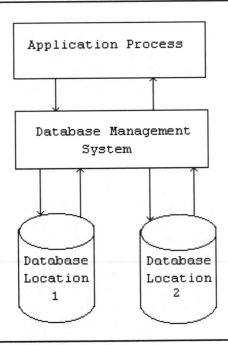

Figure 1.4   Distributed database.

1.2.4 Client/Server General Definition

The term *client / server* refers to a relationship between two systems or processes. The *client* is the system that requests work to be done on its behalf by the server system. In most situations, which is client and which is server is determined by the relationship of requester (client) to server.

Servers provide *services* to requesting clients. It is important to distinguish between servers and the services they provide. Since a single server can provide several services, the designation "server" should be carefully separated from the designation "service."

It is convenient to refer to a system or process that usually receives requests as the server and to a system or process that usually sends requests as the client. This can create some confusion, as when a server sends a request to another server. In later discussions, the context serves to distinguish clearly which type of object is being discussed.

Figure 1.5 illustrates the simple C/S relationship. The client sends a service request to the server, and the server responds with an appropriate reply.

1.2.5 Hardware Servers

It is common today to provide a variety of services from one or more networked computer systems. In this case, the machine providing the services is referred to as a server. Normally there is no end user interaction directly with the server machine. User

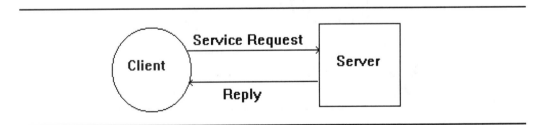

Figure 1.5   Client/server relationship.

interaction is performed with some other hardware—the hardware client—which may be a completely different type of computer and is sometimes referred to as a *work station*.

The operating system and the network software make the hardware server function. In other words, although the machine is referred to as the server, it needs specialized software to be a server.

Commonly a hardware server functions:

- As a print server, with printers attached to the servers and used by everyone on the network.
- As a file server, with common files stored on the server.
- As a storage mechanism supporting work stations that have little or no storage capacity.
- As a central storage for enterprise information.

When a hardware server is provided, it is transparent to the user and usually has little or no effect on application design. We will not discuss this type of server in the rest of this book, since the software server is what makes client/server technology so powerful.

Figure 1.6 illustrates a hardware client/server system. One

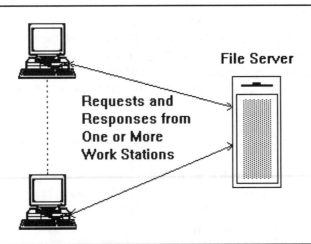

Figure 1.6   Hardware client server.

or more work stations are connected to the server and send requests to the server system. The server then responds with the required response.

1.2.6 Software Servers

Software servers are provided by special software designed specifically to handle requests. This special software is often provided on server hardware. It is not uncommon to find that the hardware provides the software server also contains the software clients.

The services provided by software servers usually fall into one of the following types:

- Data file services
- Remote procedure call services
- Database services
- Enhanced C/S capabilities, which provide a true distributed processing capability

The rest of this book will refer to software servers as simply servers.

Figure 1.7 illustrates a simple software client/server arrangement. Running programs are called *processes* in the open systems venue. The client process sends requests to the server process. The request for service names the service and includes any information required to perform it. The server performs the requested service and returns the results in the form of a reply. The client and server process may be on the same hardware system or on different hardware systems.

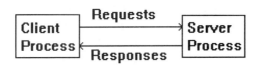

Figure 1.7   Software client/server.

1.3   TRANSACTION INTEGRITY

A *transaction* is defined as a set of actions, all of which must be completed or all of which must not be completed.

Nearly all data processing is the processing of complete transactions. Without some means of ensuring the integrity of transactions, no system could be considered useful unless there was absolute assurance there would be no failure during the processing of the transactions. In fact, in the past, failure of transactions was often discovered long after the fact, and much turmoil resulted while users attempted to restore the data integrity of the system. Modern systems decrease transactional problems enormously because they almost always include some sort of transaction management, even if the system is not built around a designated transaction processing system.

Useful application programs often update databases or perform some other type of nonreversible action. Databases are updated in order to store the latest version of data. Dispensing of funds by an automated teller is a classic nonreversible transaction. In these cases, it is essential that either all updates or actions be completed or that none be completed.

A clear example of a transaction is the teller machine. It would not be satisfactory to the customer if the account was debited unless the money is also disbursed or to the bank if the money were disbursed unless the account is also debited. An order fulfillment system is another example. It is not correct to relieve inventory of items without also updating the order database, the picking list database, and accounts receivable.

Transaction integrity, (sometimes known as *transactional integrity*) is defined as the requirement that all changes to data and all actions required by the transaction remain synchronized. Transaction integrity in a database requires that the database remain consistent with the business rules at all times. In all of the examples, the requirement for proper completion of the transaction or no action at all illustrates transaction integrity.

Transaction processing is the processing of transactions with procedures ensuring that all transactions are processed with transaction integrity. When discussing transaction processing, it is usual to call the software processes that maintain transaction integrity *transaction managers.*

All modern database products include specialized transaction managers. As we shall see later, there are also products that provide a general transaction manager, which can be used by both simple and complex application systems to ensure transaction integrity in any application, without requiring that the application programmer be aware of the intricacies of transaction management.

1.4 TYPES OF SERVERS

1.4.1 File Servers

An early, and now widespread use of servers is as *file servers.* Most networks today contain file servers, which are usually completely transparent to any user, including application developers.

File servers are supported by a combination of operating system and network manager software. In some cases, the network software makes the file server services available to the operating system in such a manner that the system has no need to be aware of the services. There are two types of file services available on many systems: file access and remote procedure call (RPC).

File access services make files on the designated hardware available to the network. The physical location of these files is generally not apparent to the user, though sometimes the user has to be signed on correctly to access particular files.

The Novell Netware file server is one popular example. It works with several operating systems but is most common with MS-DOS. In this case, the user must sign on to the server where the desired files are located. For example, a local PC may have a disc drive designated C, where files are called C:\dir1\file1. Netware servers have a mapping mechanism that maps drive designations to the local system. For instance, the local system may have a network server disc drive mapped to F. Files on it are accessed from local PCs as F:\dir\file. Developers must be aware of this designation. Application systems will provide a means so that application users need not be aware of the location of the files.

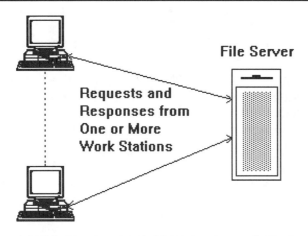

Figure 1.8   File server.

Figure 1.8 illustrates a file server. The file server, which looks very similar to a hardware server, is the simplest to understand of the C/S architectures. (In a large network using many file servers, administration and use are not always as simple as the diagram seems to indicate.) File servers are implemented by software in the network or operating system so that file access requests are routed to the server system. The server system accesses the requested file on behalf of the client system and returns a reply, which includes the result of the access.

RPC's are made available by a system that provides a library of application programs that can be accessed by other application programs as if they were simple function calls. The following C notation calls a subroutine to print information:

```
printf(\n, "Hello World");
```

Without RPC, the actual subroutine will be linked with the calling program by a system program called a *link editor*. When the main program is stored, the printf() subroutine is stored along with it, using extra disc space in each main program where printf is called. (A system called dynamic link libraries can eliminate this situa-

Figure 1.9   Simple RPC.

tion on local machines.) Using a combination of operating system services and network file server services, the program printf() may reside physically on some other machine. When the call is invoked at run time, the printf() routine may be loaded into the local machine and executed, or it may be executed on the server.

RPC technology is an evolving technology. The discussion of it in Chapter 4 will examine what is available now and what may be available in the future.

Figure 1.9 illustrates a simple RPC configuration. The application client program issues a call to a subroutine. The RPC software intercepts the call and routes it to the location of the subroutine to be executed. RPC software at the location of the subroutine is used to cause execution of the subroutine and then route the results back to the application client program.

Some simple RPC systems find the required subroutine on the remote system and transfer it back for execution to the system where the application program is executing. More sophisticated RPC systems cause the subroutine to be executed where it resides and route only the results back to the client. With simple RPC systems, subroutines are written exactly as if they were to be linked directly with the application client. Thus, neither the application developer nor the subroutine developer needs to do anything different to use the RPC system.

1.4.2 Database Servers

Major database vendors offer software features that work within networks to provide one or more database servers. Before database servers were available, all database access on a local machine required that the database reside physically on the same machine. It was very difficult, if not impossible, to access data on any machine other than where the data resided.

Database software was later designed to use file servers to store the data, but this was very costly in loss of performance and resulted in extremely high network traffic. The availability of database servers has made central and distributed storage a practical reality. Database servers and the advertising of database vendors has recently made database servers and client/server technology synonymous to many.

Database servers make database functions available on a server. File access by the database software is performed locally on the server. With database servers, the application runs on the work station, accessing the database with requests that execute database services in the server. A single database server can support a number of work stations.

Some databases provide *stored procedures,* a feature that has a limited capability to perform application functions within the database. Stored procedures provide a pseudo-distributed processing capability that can be quite powerful.

Figure 1.10 illustrates a database server. Database software

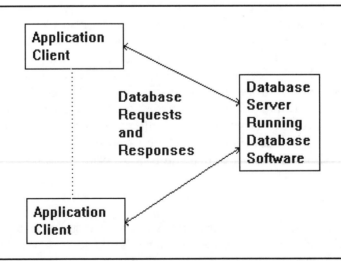

Figure 1.10   Database server.

running on the client system intercepts requests for database access and uses the network software to route the requests to the database software running on the server. Database software executes the request on the server and returns the result to the client. Since these types of systems require close cooperation between the network software and the database software, database vendors must write special software for each network system supported.

1.4.3   Enhanced Client/Server Processing

Enhanced C/S processing adds the following features:

- Application servers may be placed on any system in the network.
- The load is automatically balanced among several servers performing the same service.
- Multiple application servers may be active on the same or multiple machines.
- Requests may be routed to a particular server, depending on the data passed with the request.
- Application programs are never aware of the locations of services invoked.
- Multiple database types (heterogeneous databases) can be used in the system with a minimal programming effort.
- New types of databases may be added, or existing database types may be changed with little or no impact on application programs.

There are a number of additional features provided by such systems. These will be described in Chapter 7.

Enhanced client/server processing is provided by distributed transaction processing systems. It is unfortunate that many people think of transaction processing as a specific requirement: in fact, all programs that update databases are performing transaction processing.

Figure 1.11 illustrates enhanced client/server technology. One or more clients issue requests for service that are intercepted by the name server. The name server routes the request to the appro-

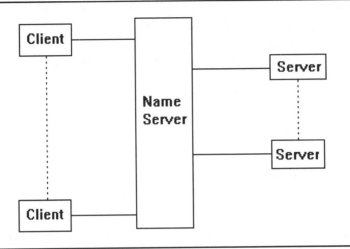

Figure 1.11   Enhanced client/server.

priate server based on the name of the service and other considerations. The server performs the requested service and returns the
response to the client. Multiple servers may provide the same service. The name server provides several methods to determine
which server to use including data-dependent routing and load
balancing. Both methods may be changed by administrative services without affecting the operation of the clients or servers.

1.5   RPC, PEER-TO-PEER, AND CONVERSATIONAL

In addition to the traditional RPC client/server relationship between two computer processes are two other paradigms for cooperative distributed computing: conversational and peer-to-peer.

The *conversational paradigm* allows a process to initiate a
conversation with another process. The two processes may then
exchange a number of messages, and either process may terminate the conversation. There are limitations to conversational
processing. One is that a process may be involved in no more
than one conversation at a time, so both processes are tied up
with each other until the process is complete. Neither can respond to attempts by other processes to communicate.

The initiating process and the server process remain in a client/server relationship. The server provides services to the client and maintains full context of what has gone before in the conversation while the conversation is proceeding. When the conversation is complete, the server loses all information about the conversation. Usually the server is a *daemon* that does not go away at the end of the conversation, but rather makes itself available to provide service to the next conversation requested (which may be from the same process as previously).

Figure 1.12 illustrates the conversational paradigm. Process 1 initiates a conversation with process 2 and exchanges a number of messages (while both processes maintain information on what has gone before in the conversation [the context]). Then process 1 terminates the conversation. Process 2 loses context of the conversation and becomes ready to serve other processes that may need its services. Conversational capabilities are provided by some enhanced client/server products such as TUXEDO.

The *peer-to-peer paradigm* supports communication between independent processes. Using peer-to-peer communications, any process may initiate a message exchange with any other process at any time. As many messages as desired may be exchanged on any of several peer-to-peer connections by either process, and peer-to-peer processes may each maintain message exchanges with as many other processes as desired.

When the peer-to-peer exchange is closed, both processes may

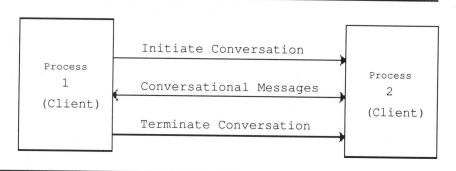

Figure 1.12   Conversational paradigm.

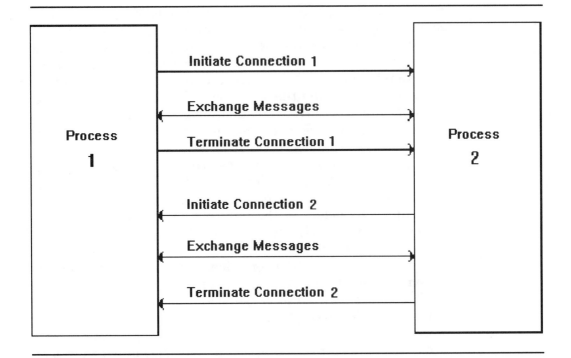

Figure 1.13   Peer-to-peer paradigm.

continue independently and may initiate another peer-to-peer exchange with each other or with other processes. Both processes can maintain context of their processing after completing a peer-to-peer exchange, and therefore another connection can be established that depends on previous communications.

Figure 1.13 illustrates the peer-to-peer paradigm. Process 1 initiates a peer-to-peer connection with process 2, exchanges messages, and terminates the connection. Both process 1 and process 2 may maintain context of the exchange during and after the connection is broken down. In the illustration, process 2 later initiates a peer-to-peer connection with process 1, exchanges messages, and then ends the connection. Again both processes may maintain context during and after the connection is broken down. Note that both process 1 and process 2 could also have open peer-to-peer connections with other processes while exchanging messages with each other.

One product that provides peer-to-peer capabilities is the LU6.2 Advanced Program-to-Program Communications (APPC) provided by IBM on many of its platforms. APPC also provides many communication capabilities, including conversational and client/server, RPC-like functionality.

2

Planning for Client/Server

2.1 GENERAL CONSIDERATIONS

Client/server technology supports many modern business initiatives, from empowering users to saving on computing costs. The benefits seem obvious, and many users have rushed to install client/server, only to fail to get the anticipated results. The reasons they often cite for this failure include the following:

- "The technology is not mature."
- "There is not enough knowledge about the technology."
- "Client/server simply doesn't work in that environment."
- "The tools we used to have on the mainframe do not exist or don't work well enough."

In fact, most of these failures resolve to the following actual reasons:

- There was incomplete or no planning.
- Personnel were not properly trained.
- The people who chose the software did not understand the implications of running applications in a distributed environment and chose products on the basis of market hype.

As a result of incomplete planning and misunderstanding of the capabilities of the products available, the wrong software or hardware, or both, was purchased, and the resulting system could not support the expectations of the organization.

This chapter examines of the technical factors that should be used in planning for a client/server system. (Later chapters provide details about various types of client/server systems and examine the capabilities inherent in each.) No matter what claims the vendor makes, the purchaser must verify that the system will behave in the specific required environment and provide the results expected.

2.2   REASONS FOR USING CLIENT/SERVER

Most organizations that are planning to install new computer systems should consider client/server technology, but a client/server system should not be installed just because it seems like a good idea or because other organizations are giving glowing reports about their success. Client/server systems bring their own set of problems. Simply replacing an existing system with a client/server system may exacerbate problems.

Careful planning is at the heart of any successful effort. When introducing new technology to an organization, planning properly, with full understanding of the implications of each choice, is the only way to prevent potential disaster.

An enterprise should consider using client/server if some combination of the following conditions exists:

- Many people are to have access to computer records and processing.
- There is a need to use the power of work stations to interact with users intelligently to make it easier to use the information in the computer.
- Instant access to information is needed if people are to do their work effectively.
- Those needing access to the enterprise database are in multiple locations.
- There is a need to maintain a central database.

- There is a need for local smaller databases, that are current, not copied from the central database the night before.
- People are setting up databases for their own use and getting complacent about maintaining the central database.
- The business is growing, and is expected to continue to grow, requiring ever-expanding computing power.
- The computer system must be available when needed, with downtime minimized.

A properly designed client/server system can support a growing business, large or small, with reasonable initial cost and minimal maintenance expense.

2.3   WHAT THE SYSTEM SHOULD PROVIDE

A client/server system has these hardware components:

- Work stations
- Hardware servers
- Data storage devices, (usually disks attached to the servers and work stations)
- Networking hardware

Hardware choices should be made after the requirements of the system have been analyzed and the software is selected. The hardware chosen should run the software the most efficiently at the lowest total cost. Other factors to consider are its reliability, service and maintenance requirements, expansion capabilities, and vendor reputation.

Because the effectiveness of a computer system depends on the software, this chapter concentrates on it. It is extremely important that the business requirements are analyzed and the proper software choices made before the hardware is decided on. Properly chosen software will open up a large number of hardware choices and will tend to prevent the organization's getting locked in to some specific hardware.

Once an organization has decided to use a client/server system, it must then define the essential requirements for the system. The requirements may include many factors, but they must include the following information:

- The number of users who will be signed onto the system at any given time.
- The probable number of users who will be actively using the system at the same time (as opposed to those who are signed on but idle).
- The size of the database in bytes and number of rows or records.
- The number and types of transactions per second that must be supported by the system.
- The requirement for data and transaction integrity. (Would it be satisfactory for one file or table to be updated but not another if the system fails during a transaction?)
- The amount of data likely to be needed to process the required application systems.
- The time allowed for a user to wait for the system to respond to a request (response time).

After the basic information is gathered, these questions must be addressed?

- Will these requirements expand very much before the cost of the system is amortized?
- What will it cost to expand the system, and will reprogramming be required to do so?
- What will be the cost to develop applications with the proposed software?

Vendors are not always candid about the capabilities of their systems. They must be asked to provide complete answers to questions about how their products support each of the identified needs. Use the information in this book to evaluate vendor responses, and be sure to get answers to the following questions:

- What type of load will the proposed applications put on the network using this software?
- What will happen to the programs when more servers are

added and the database is distributed differently? Will they need to change?
- How many concurrent users will the software support on various hardware configurations?
- If new and better hardware becomes available, what will be the cost to convert the software?
- Does the system fully support transaction integrity? What implications does this support have for application developers?

Most vendors will state that their system will meet all needs presented. The people with the responsibility for choosing must be able to evaluate the actual implications of using each proposed software approach.

2.4 PITFALLS TO AVOID

2.4.1 Overloading the Network

Any network must be considered a limited resource. The *bandwidth,* or capacity to carry data, is finite. Network bandwidth can be expanded only by spending more money, which is also a limited resource. Therefore, care must be taken not to treat the network as a magic transfer mechanism and simply plan on sending however many messages of whatever size is convenient.

Organizations should be especially careful of products sold by vendors to be client/server solutions but that merely provide support for applications to run on the workstation, using the server computer only to provide data. These systems treat the network as a simple input/output (I/O) device and tend to place many messages of various sizes on the network.

Systems that use relational databases are especially vulnerable to overloading the network. Because the relational database on the server performs many processes that are part of application requirements, they certainly decrease the network load when compared with simple file servers. Many people feel that by using the relational database in the server, the system has reached the point where it can support many users. Unfortunately, unless the bandwidth of the network is very high (expensive), the network will saturate at many fewer users than advertised.

Note that the problem is that work station–based products, variously advertised as "object oriented," 4GL, and "client/server application generator," must perforce use generalized Structured Query Language (SQL) statements to access the relational database. As a consequence, they tend to send many requests over the network, receiving relatively raw data in return, which is then processed in the work station.

If the number of users is relatively low then these tools provide a means to create applications at relatively low cost. If the number of users is likely to grow, other approaches, such as enhanced client/server products, must be considered.

2.4.2   Failure to Maintain Transaction Integrity

Some of the more common complaints about client/server technology include problems with maintaining the various parts of the database in synchronization. This loss of synchronization is usually the result of not using software that guarantees transactional integrity.

Popular relational databases include transaction management in the form of the SQL COMMIT WORK statement. If the database is from a single vendor and uses the vendor's distribution software, such as Oracle's SQL*NET, then transaction integrity is protected (as long as the application follows the rules provided by the vendor). If, on the other hand, the application is built on some other type of distribution software, such as the popular bridges or some client/server development tools, then the enterprise must be very careful to determine if and how the software maintains transaction integrity.

Some bridges and object oriented client/server development tools support distributed databases as follows:

- A log is kept of all changes to the databases
- When the transaction is committed, the software commits each database individually
- If any commit fails, the log is used to reverse the updates

This method works fine when there is only one user making changes. When there is another user, it is possible that changes might be made to an already committed database before the reversal has started. Then, when the reversal is done, the second set of updates are lost. The probably of this loss occurring rising exponentially with the number of users on the system that will be making changes to the databases.

2.4.3   Loss of Security

Whenever networks are added, especially when there is a complex interlocking network, security can be more easily compromised. In most cases, simple sign-on and the GRANT type security mechanisms become much less effective. Every organization that uses client/server should carefully determine security requirements and make sure that they are met by the software and hardware used. Some companies that install large client/server systems have found that they must develop their own security systems and standards, perhaps using systems such as Kerberos.

In any case, no enterprise can afford to take security for granted just because a security mechanism is supplied with the purchased tools and supporting software. Many have complained that the security mechanisms available for client/server are weak and they have been hurt by security breaches.

2.4.4   Wrong Sizing the Platforms

Some have complained about the unexpected high cost of client/ server systems. Many times the cost goes above budget because the system was designed with the wrong size platforms for the type of software and the number of users in the system.

One particularly bad case occurred when a government agency set up a local area network (LAN) running custom software built on a popular database. It supplied every user with a fast computer with high-speed disk as a work station, and used a slower platform with slower disks as a server. With a high-speed LAN and about 20 users, the system crashed intermittently, leaving the agency unable to perform its work reliably. This system was created as a result of a number of false assumptions:

- Since the server was required only to do database operations, it would not have much load.

- Since the work stations were running the application code, they would need to be fast.
- Since the server was doing only database operations and the vendor gave them a lower price, they put the application code on the server and the work stations had to download the code (with many overlays) as operations continued

The problem was compounded because the software had been specified by a central agency, which expected the server to be the faster system, using smaller computers as work stations. As originally specified, the vendor was required to create software to operate in 640K of memory, so there were a large number of overlays. Office politics also played a role. In order to correct the problem, the department ordered a larger machine to use as a server, and it was delivered instead to a person with more office perks who was not even on the system.

To choose a client/server system that is the right size the load on both the servers and the work stations must be analyzed. The more users, the larger and faster the server must be, up to the point at which the network is saturated. Generally any modern work station need not be the largest and fastest unless there are specific requirements for the extra power. Remember that more power in the work stations seldom removes load from the server.

2.4.5   Lack of Scalability

Scalability is the ability to increase the amount of computing resources available to run an application with minimum impact on the application software and minimum administrative effort. The measure of scalability is somewhat subjective, but to be scalable, the system must have at least the following characteristics:

- Adding new servers with computer platforms of the same type as already in use should have no effect on application programs; that is, it must require no program changes, no recompiling of programs, and no relinking of programs.
- The underlying support software should require no changes or reinstallation on the existing platforms.

- Administrative changes to existing system definitions should be minimal.

Adding a server platform that can run the same executables as already exist should require no more than the following effort:

- Installing and setting up the new platform.
- Redistributing the data.
- Copying application programs to the new system.
- Adding the definition of the new system to the administrative control files of the existing system.
- Defining routing of service requests to the new system.

If the new server is a platform that is not capable of running existing executables, the only additional step required should be recompiling the application programs on the new platform.

Some client/server application development tools claim that there is no need to recompile the application to move to a different machine type. These systems work functionally, but they must run interpretively (every statement is parsed and compiled, then executed one by one as the application is run), causing poor performance.

Some enterprises have installed a system and made it work very well, but then found that they could not expand capacity without major rework of the application systems. This problem is sometimes compounded by a failure of the development system to move easily to new, more efficient platforms without major efforts to reinstall all existing support software.

2.4.6 Poor Performance

Modern enterprises depend on computers for mission critical information-intensive operations. Computer systems users must have accurate information quickly if they are to be productive. Yet performance where it counts—at the end user—is perhaps the least measured factor in managing costs. If the system is sluggish and causes a few seconds of extra wait on each use, the loss in productivity can be staggering. For example, if 100 people are using the system and they must wait an extra few seconds on each transaction during the day (this wait is a time of complete idleness), the total loss can reach ten minutes each day for each person. The total loss is over 16 person-hours lost each day because of slow computer response. This calculation is based on 100 transactions per day, with a loss of six seconds with each transaction. The importance of performance cannot be overstated.

Poor performance may be one of the most vexing problems complained about by those who have installed client/server systems. Among the many reasons why performance does not come up to expectations are these common ones:

- The support software, such as an object-oriented development tool, put too much data on the network, causing slow network response.
- The support software starts too many processes in the server, causing the server to spend too many central processing unit (CPU) cycles switching from process to process.
- All processing is done in the work station, causing poor performance unless more expensive work stations are installed.
- The database is not properly defined to maximize performance.

Some highly publicized client/server development tools start a process in the server for every user on the system. Most operating systems, UNIX particularly, use CPU cycles to switch from process to process. The number of cycles used rises exponentially with the number of processes that are available to run. When a few processes are involved, adding one more makes little difference, but if there are hundreds of users and each has a dedicated process on the server, the server will often become busy with simply process switching. Adding computer power helps but does not correct the underlying problem. Client/server systems should have a way to reuse processes started in the server. Further, there should be an administrative feature that allows control of the number of processes started.

When all the processing is done in the work station, using the server only as a database server, it requires more computing power in the work station. Some companies have planned their client/server systems using smaller, lower-priced work stations and have suffered slow processing times. The work load must be balanced between the work stations and the servers to achieve the desired price-performance ratios.

If the database is not distributed among the disk storage devices properly, a large amount of head movement will be required for each transaction. When this occurs, performance can suffer heavily. The chosen database should allow easy tuning of data distribution over the available disk, and the combination of the client/server software and the database software should allow changing the data distribution without great effort, with easy placement of data.

3

General Information on Networks and Platforms

3.1 SOME TERMS

The following terms are used extensively in this and following chapters and must be understood: *protocol, bandwidth,* and *saturation.*

A *protocol* is a set of rules enforced by the system to ensure correct results. Networks use special protocols to guarantee that the data sent arrives at the destination accurately. The protocol between a client and server is simple:

- The client may request service at any time.
- The server must be ready to receive the request.
- The server may communicate with the client only in response to a service request.

In reality, the client/server protocol sometimes allows the server to communicate with the client while processing the request. This ability can be used to return interim results or to notify the client of a problem while processing. This type of protocol addition complicates the client because it requires the client to be ready to receive messages from a server at any time after sending the request.

The *bandwidth* of a network is its capacity to carry data. LAN bandwidths are usually measured in millions of bits per second, or megabits per second (Mb). Wide area networks (WANs) are usually measured in thousands of bits per second, or kilobits per second(Kb).

A network becomes *saturated* when its capacity to move data has been reached. Often when the volume of data approaches the capacity of the network, the network becomes saturated with its own overhead and cannot send the number of bits per second that the network specifications say.

3.2   MS-DOS SERVERS

3.2.1   Typical Hardware

A typical MS-DOS based server hardware configuration is shown in Figure 3.1.

The server will have sufficient power and disk storage to support the network user needs. Some configuration possibilities are these

- Multiple CPUs
- Multiple gigabytes of disk

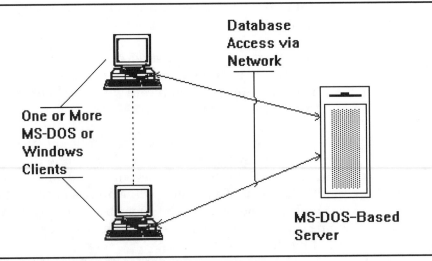

Figure 3.1   MS-DOS client/server configuration.

- High processing power, such as Intel Pentium CPUs
- Sixteen or more megabytes of random access memory (RAM).

Some configurations contain multiple servers. Under some conditions of use, multiple single CPU servers with less disk storage, such as 500MB, will serve the network users better than providing a single server with high power and large storage. Multiple servers work well when:

- Some protection against server failure is required, since failure of a single server out of several is less of a problem than the failure of a single, more powerful server.
- Databases are smaller and can be distributed easily among the various servers
- There are multiple applications that allow databases supporting the various applications to be placed on different servers.

The clients will be MS-DOS systems and will most likely be configured with Windows. The client hardware configuration will typically be:

- Single CPU
- Moderate-rate processing power, such as single Intel 80486DX CPUs running at 33 MHz or 40 MHz (in some cases, the lower-cost 80386 or 80486SX work quite satisfactorily)
- 100 to 200 MB of disk

3.2.2 The Operating System

MS-DOS does not easily support multiple users. Therefore, network products load another layer on top of MS-DOS to do most of the operating system functions and manage multiple users. MS-DOS remains as a sort of background task to provide MS-DOS features as required. The network operating system features may include these:

- Multitasking to allow several users to be logged on and using the system

- Multiprocessing to take advantage of multiple CPUs if present (provided by some network systems, such as Novell Netware and Banyon Vines)
- Network addressing and management
- Network administration
- Network security

3.3   UNIX SERVERS

3.3.1   Typical Hardware

A typical UNIX based server hardware configuration is shown in Figure 3.2.

The server will have considerable power to support a large number of users, each with frequent access for complex uses. Some configuration possibilities are:

- Multiple gigabytes of disk
- Very high processing power
- 64 MB or more of RAM

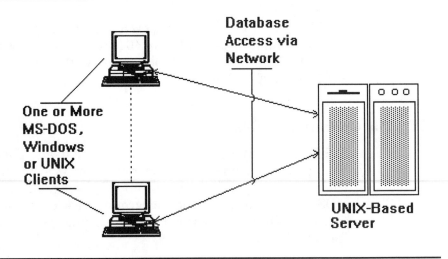

Figure 3.2   UNIX client/server configuration.

The actual disk space will depend on user needs. UNIX platforms support very large disk capacity.

The processing power will come from one or all of the following:

- Parallel processing with symmetric multiprocessing (SMP) implemented partially in hardware, with up to 24 or more processors
- Modern computer chips with relatively large internal cache, using very high clock rates
- Very high speed internal bus

UNIX is able to manage the large amount of RAM necessary to support very high processing power. It is also capable of supporting smaller servers when the large computing power is not required. A server configured as follows can be very useful and still provide the power and flexibility of UNIX at a relatively low cost:

- Moderate processing power, such as single Intel Pentium or equivalent CPU
- One gigabyte of disk, or even less if it serves user needs
- 16 MB of RAM

Applications developed on UNIX can be moved relatively easily to new platforms that also use UNIX, in most cases requiring only recompiling and relinking the application programs.

A UNIX server system can support multiple server platforms in the network. The considerations for using multiple smaller systems as servers instead of a single large system are the same as for MS-DOS, except that UNIX supports both smaller and larger systems.

With UNIX, it is possible to install a configuration with no designated server system, where data is shared by all, but stored in individual work stations. In this case, protection against failure becomes optimal, since each platform contains only a small portion of the data and represents a small part of the computing power in the network.

There are some problems to be solved when not using a designated server system:

- Central control of data is more difficult.
- Administration of the system becomes more important.
- Security of data becomes more difficult.
- The location of data becomes more critical, yet is more difficult to control.

Some advantages of not using a central server are these:

- Cost may be lower, since only work stations are required.
- Data can often be located so that access is usually local, lowering the load on the network.
- Database software generally is designed to operate in a specified server platform.

Later chapters describe some of the methods that will allow better control of the network system and make administration of distributed systems easier. One major difficulty with distributed systems is managing partitioned database tables, a subject covered in Chapter 7.

3.3.2   The Operating System

UNIX, as it stands, supports networking, including multitasking and background network server processes, called *listeners*. The general term often used to refer to such background tasks is *daemons*.

Networking software for UNIX servers provides protocol enforcement and addressing and transmitting/receiving functions. They are part of the transport layer in the International Standards Organization (ISO)—Open Systems Interconnection (OSI) model.

4

File Servers

4.1 TYPICAL HARDWARE

A file server system typically has the following components:

- One or more computers with relatively large disk capacity, usually called *servers*.
- Smaller computers, usually called *work stations,* at users' desks.
- Communications equipment.

The servers may use any type of operating system—for example, MS-DOS, Windows, Windows/NT, UNIX, or OS/2. If a server uses MS-DOS,the network software creates another layer on top of MS-DOS, which takes over most operating system functions. This layer serves a number of purposes but is there primarily to provide multitasking so that multiple users can use the server.

The work stations may also use any of the operating systems noted. Often the operating system on the work stations is the same type as on the server. If the server is an MS-DOS platform, then, in general, the work stations must also be MS-DOS platforms. If the server is UNIX, the work stations may be UNIX, OS/2, or MS-DOS platforms. If the server is an OS/2 platform, then the work stations generally must be either MS-DOS or OS/2 plat-forms.

4.2   NETWORK REQUIREMENTS

4.2.1   Overview

The primary requirement for networks supporting file servers is data capacity. In general, networks for file servers require a high bandwidth. The usual file server request calls for large volumes of data. Since the sole purpose of a file server is to provide data storage, all data is processed at the work station, requiring that the work station acquire the needed data from the server. Using diskless work stations can require very high bandwidths to pro-vide reasonable performance.

A typical capacity for an LAN is 10 Mb. Higher-speed LANs, especially those using fiber-optic methods, can reach very high speeds—on the order of 50 Mb or more. A WAN from a telephone company begins with 56 Kb. The telephone company will increase this capacity as much as a customer is willing to pay for, but at high cost.

The capacity designation for a network can be misleading. Generally LANs require about 30 percent of the stated capacity to carry protocol information. WANs usually require less—often about 10 percent. Additionally, some LANs cannot carry the stated capacity because they become overloaded with overhead processing well below the stated speed. This overhead is caused by a number of circumstances but usually is most affected by the number of messages on the line.

When considering the acquisition of a network for supporting file servers, it is important to consider the nature of the data, the number of users, the type of work station, the frequency of access by each user, and network characteristics.

4.2.2   Nature of the Data

The nature of the data refers to such items as the source code used for development, files for production system data storage, and RPCs.

If source code used for development is stored on a file server, an important consideration is whether these files will remain on the server while modifications are made and compiles run or whether the source code will be downloaded to the work station for actual development work and returned to the file server when development is complete. Since compilers use a lot of file I/O, when several developers are using the same network a large amount of traffic can be generated if compiles are run using source and work files on the server. For this reason, file servers supporting software development should be connected with very high bandwidth networks.

If the file server is supporting production systems, then consideration must be given to the use of the files on the server. If the server stores files that are accessed only occasionally, such as control files loaded at the beginning of processing, the traffic on the network may not be very heavy. But if all files used by the system are stored on the server and all processing is done at the work stations, then the traffic can become very heavy, especially at peak usage times.

If the file server is being used to support RPC, the traffic on the network depends on the nature and use of the RPC library by the work station programs. For instance, if the server library contains only common subroutines used occasionally by the work stations, the network traffic may not exceed reasonable limits. If all subroutines are stored on the server, then simply running programs on the work station may place a heavy load on the network.

4.2.3   Number of Simultaneous Users

The number of users directly affects the network requirements. In general, once the nature of the data and its access requirements are determined for the typical user, the network bandwidth requirement can be determined by multiplying the requirement for the typical user by the number of simultaneous users. Also, most network systems require some overhead to support a user signed onto the network. For this reason, it is important to examine the network being considered for the amount of this overhead, since it can cause some surprises.

4.2.4   Type of Work Station

The type of work station is either a diskless work station or a work station that has local disk storage. The consideration is whether most, if not all, files will be loaded onto the local work station for processing with occasional updating of the central storage. Often if the work stations contain sufficient storage and there is little or no updating of the server from the work station, the traffic can be relatively light. At the other extreme, diskless work stations will perform all data access at the server, causing considerable traffic.

4.2.5   Frequency of Access

The frequency of access from each user at a work station has a direct bearing on the traffic requirements of the network. If each work station accesses the server infrequently, the total traffic will be less. Usually the frequency of access depends to a large extent on the type of use given the work station. If users remain logged on with infrequent use, then the load is obviously less than if the user is constantly using the work station to access files on the server.

4.2.6   Network Characteristics

To get satisfactory performance from the network, the characteristics of the network protocol and type must be considered. Peak loads more than 75 percent of the total capacity may cause severe degradation of the network throughput. Token ring networks are particularly prone to saturation at much less than total capacity. Many other network types can perform well up to nearly full capacity without adverse effect on performance. The network architect and planner must be sure that sufficient capacity is present to prevent peak load saturation for the type of network installed.

4.3   HOW MS-DOS FILE SERVERS WORK

Figure 4.1 illustrates a typical MS-DOS file server system. There can be multiple DOS work stations using the server.

The server starts as a plain MS-DOS system. When the net-

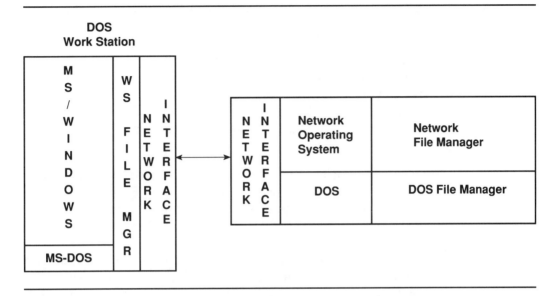

Figure 4.1   DOS file server.

work server software system is installed, this software takes over nearly all the functions of the operating system; hence, it is often called the network operating system. On the server, the system has several main logical components:

- The network operating system, which manages the resources of the machine and directs the work to the appropriate location.
- The network interface, which interfaces with the communications equipment.
- The network file manager, which manages remote access requests.
- MS-DOS, which is usually quiet when the network operating system is being used.
- The MS-DOS file manager, which is sometimes used by the network file manager to access the actual physical files.

The MS-DOS work station has the following software components installed:

- MS-DOS, which remains the operating system for the work station.
- Windows, which, if installed, operates in the normal manner but configured for network usage.
- The work station file manager, which is provided as part of the network software and intercepts network file access. The manager is installed as a device driver for file access.
- The network interface, which interfaces with the communications equipment.

The work station may have physical drives A, B, C, and D; the server or servers are assigned virtual drives E, F, through Z. The process of assigning virtual drives is called *mapping*. From the user's viewpoint, the virtual drives are used in the same way as the local physical drives.

When file access is requested by a program running on the work station, the work station file manager intercepts the request and examines the drive portion of the path. If the request is for a local physical drive, the request is passed to MS-DOS for normal processing. If the request is for a drive on a server, the request is passed via the communications network to the server.

When a request for file access is received by the server, the network operating system invokes the network file manager, which translates the virtual drive into a physical drive on the server and passes the request to the DOS file manager.

The MS-DOS file manager performs the request (read, write, delete, etc.) and passes the result to the network operating system, which creates a message containing the information and passes the message to the network interface, which places the message on the network.

When the message is received at the work station, the network interface formats the data in the message into standard MS-DOS I/O format and returns the information to the requesting program via MS-DOS or Windows.

The MS-DOS or Windows program can use the virtual drives exactly as if they were local drives and receive the results without consideration for the source of the access.

4.4   HOW UNIX FILE SERVERS WORK

UNIX file servers are platforms dedicated to providing disk access for the network. UNIX networks provide access through a number of systems, variously called network file system (NFS) or remote file system (RFS).

NFS, the more comprehensive, providing the means not only to support file servers but to make all files on all UNIX platforms in the network available to all other systems in the network. UNIX networked file systems usually also make DOS files, including files on DOS machines, available to the network, though this is not always implemented on given systems. This discussion will be limited to all UNIX networks.

Figure 4.2 shows the components of an application program that uses NFS. The application program accesses files using function calls that access the UNIX *kernel,* which passes the file access

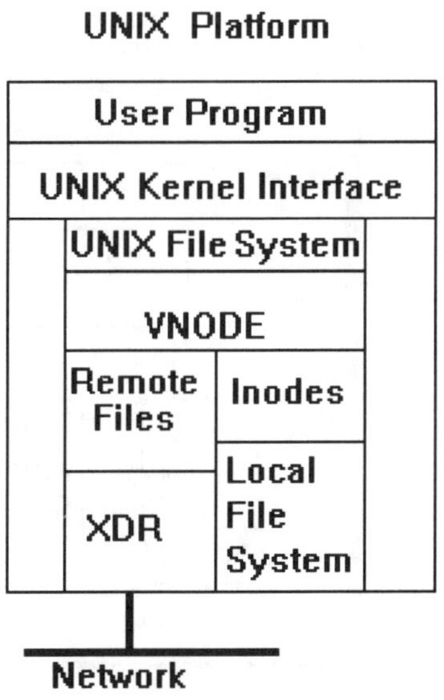

UNIX Platform

| User Program |
| UNIX Kernel Interface |

UNIX File System	
VNODE	
Remote Files	Inodes
	Local File System
XDR	

Network

Figure 4.2   Network file system on a UNIX platform.

request to the UNIX file system. The application programmer does not need to make any provision in the program for NFS. The functions in the network libraries provide all necessary connections.

UNIX includes a feature in its file system called *inodes,* a data structure containing all the information required to access a given local file. NFS inserts a set of vnodes between the kernel and the inodes. A *vnode,* or virtual inode, is a data structure containing the information required to locate all files in the system.

A vnode keys on the highest node in the path assigned to a physical disk. That is, given the path /user/myfiles/filename, the description "user" is attached by the system to a physical area on some disk in the network. Using the information in the vnode (Figure 4.3), the NFS function known as virtual file system (VFS)

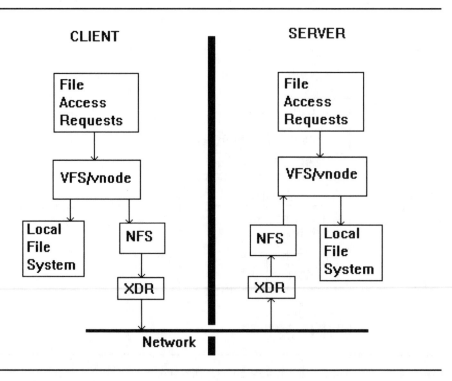

Figure 4.3   UNIX file server flow.

passes the access request to the proper system. If "user" is local, NFS will pass the request to the local file system, which will use its inode set to access the requested file. If "user" is remote, NFS will address the request to the proper platform and send the request via the network.

NFS has the capability to address platforms with various data representations, so it uses a function called *XDR* to translate the data in the message to a standard format before placing the message on the network. XDR will be used on the receiving platform to translate the data to the correct format for that platform. If all systems in the network have the same data representation, NFS may be set up to bypass the use of XDR to increase performance.

Figure 4.3 illustrates the flow of NFS file access requests. The file access calls from the application flow to VFS, which examines the vnodes to find the location of the file.

4.5   REMOTE PROCEDURE CALLS

4.5.1   Definition of Remote Procedure Calls

All useful programs use subroutines to accomplish their function. The invocation of a subroutine is called a *function call*. It is obvious in languages such as C when subroutines are used. It is not so obvious that all languages, even the most advanced 4GL, use function calls extensively.

RPC provides the capability for any program to use function calls to execute subroutines without regard for the location of the subroutine. That is, the program executes the subroutine in the exact same way whether the function is hard linked with the program or is stored separately on another machine, perhaps a file server.

4.5.2   How RPCs Work

After a program has been compiled, a procedure called a *link edit* is run to connect the main part of the program with the functions it has called. When the link edit is run and RPC is not going to be used, one of the following will occur:

- Each subroutine is linked with the application executable code such that it is loaded with the main program and resides in core exactly as if it is a part of the main program. This is called a *hard link*. A program with hard-linked functions is illustrated in Figure 4.4.
- Each subroutine is linked with a mechanism that loads the subroutine only when required and may be swapped out of memory. This is called a *dynamic link*.

Hard links work in the same way on any operating system. In a single system without a network, dynamic function calls on MS-DOS are available using special tools, called *linkers,* available from several vendors. windows provides for dynamic linking using the *dynamic-link library (DLL)* feature. And UNIX provides for dynamic linking using the *dynamic library* feature. Windows DLLs and UNIX dynamic library features allow sharing of a single copy of a subroutine. Figure 4.5 illustrates dynamic function calls.

An all-MS-DOS network can provide RPC capability to an MS-DOS client if special libraries are provided on the client.

Application Program

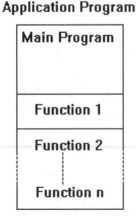

Figure 4.4   Hard-linked functions.

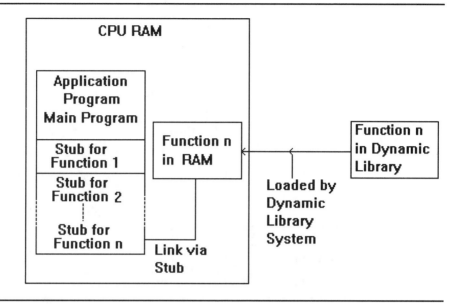

Figure 4.5   Dynamic link.

These special libraries contain special versions of the functions available for use via RPC. These special versions look exactly like the ordinary version of the function to the application, but instead of actually being the function, they invoke the network to access the desired function at the server and then execute it on the server. This capability is the basis for database servers and will be discussed in more detail in a later chapter.

Windows provides for a neater approach to RPC than DOS. Since the DLL is already dynamically retrieved and executed when needed, all that happens is that the request to load the DLL is treated like any other file read process. Windows is rarely aware that it is loading the DLL from the server instead of locally. All DLLs are executed in the client. Since a DLL, once loaded, is retained in memory until that memory is needed for some other purpose, clients running Windows applications on a network with DLLs stored on the file server should have as much local memory as possible to minimized network traffic. Figure 4.6 illustrates how DLL RPC works.

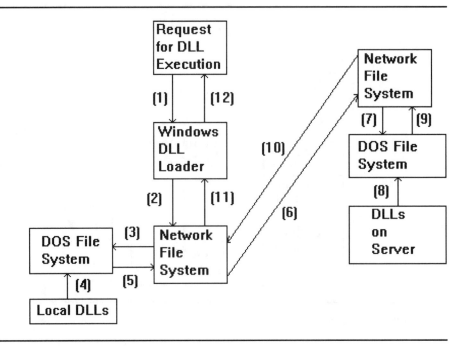

Figure 4.6   Dynamic link library remote procedure call.

DLLs may call functions to be executed on the server. Again, discussion on this subject is deferred to the examination of database servers.

There are a number of schemes used with UNIX to implement RPC. The simplest is described here and is based on dynamic library usage. Figure 4.7 illustrates the flow for RPC using dynamic libraries and NFS.

The function call request is handled initially by a special stub for dynamic libraries placed in the calling program by the link editor. The stub will load the function from the designated library using standard system file requests and then execute the function and return the result to the calling program. As the diagram shows, the file access requests are handled by NFS in the same manner as for any other file request. The link editor

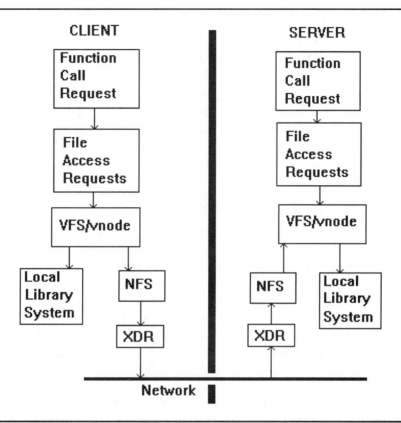

Figure 4.7   UNIX remote procedure call with dynamic libraries.

chooses the library when it is run, using instructions given to it by the programmer.

More elaborate RPC schemes provide the following features:

- Allow the calling program to be unaware of the RPC in the same manner as dynamic libraries.
- Allow the calling program to be written specifically to cause the function to be loaded from a specific library.
- Cause the function to be executed at the server instead of being moved to the client before execution.

4.6 APPLICATION DESIGN CONSIDERATIONS

In general, programs function with file servers exactly as they did with local files, except the network and shared server platform introduce the following considerations:

- Performance changes caused by moving data over the network.
- The performance capabilities of the server.
- Transaction integrity at greater risk due to a higher possibility of failure because of the network

4.6.1 Performance Considerations

Usually application systems are not designed specifically to meet the characteristics of file server networks. Instead, applications are designed for local operation, and the network is configured to meet the performance needs. Often this calls for increased bandwidth, larger servers, and more servers as the load on the system increases. There are very few methods to prevent file server system resource requirements from rapidly expanding, especially if the system contains diskless clients. The following suggestions can help, even with diskless clients:

- Whenever possible, use RPC capabilities to run programs in the server, with the main program in the client performing the human interaction function.
- Provide sufficient RAM in the client to download large blocks of data to the client, where it can be processed with less access to the server.
- Run the part of the application that accesses data in the server to decrease the network traffic. Since most client/server networks have limited bandwidth, these techniques can improve performance considerably. The downside is that the load on the server is increased. If the application designer is aware of the server capabilities and use frequency, the design can be tailored to optimize the compromise between network load and server load. In some cases, it may be more economical to increase server capacity instead of network capacity.

Increasing RAM capacity in clients can decrease the load on the network by allowing large blocks of data to be downloaded for processing in the client. Generally this approach does not affect server requirements but can lower the network traffic, especially at peak times. In some applications, downloaded data can be stored longer, requiring less access to the disk files on the server. If the data is relatively static, it can be held in the client for a relatively long time, accessing the server only to obtain updated information.

These techniques also can complicate application development, and they must be carefully considered in this light. It is also true that most 4GLs and object-oriented languages do not include an ability to make these application-dependent decisions.

If clients in the system include local disk storage, it may be possible to use the server only to contain central data, with all local data stored at the client. In this case, then even more consideration should be given to processing centralized data in the server to reduce traffic on the network, and performing processing of local data in the client.

The trend is to ignore these considerations and aim for higher bandwidth in the network as well as providing larger capacity in the servers. Each installation—development cost, performance requirements, and future expansion needs—must be considered individually.

4.6.2 Transaction Integrity

If a program updates more than one file while processing and it is important that the work done to all updated files be maintained in synchronization, then transaction integrity becomes important. When using a file server for either direct file access or RPC, it is very difficult to protect against loss of transaction integrity in the network while the program is running.

Transaction integrity is lost when a program has updated some files but has not yet completed the update to other files when the system fails, causing the program to halt. Complete protection can be provided only by using a transaction management function.

Some protection can be obtained by minimizing the time between the start of the first file update and the completion of the last file update. A program that requires at least a minimum of protection against loss of transaction integrity should perform all update activities after the transaction is otherwise complete. The following C segment illustrates the point:

```
/* This coding example is in C                    */
.
.
.
/* all processing before updating files has       */
/* been done by this point                        */

if(err1 = (update1, parm11 . . . .))
{
/* put error handling here */
}
/* if update1 fails and the following updates are    */
/* done, transaction integrity will be lost          */
if(err2 = (update2, parm21 . . . .))
{
/* put error handling here */
}
/* if update1 succeeds and either update2 or update3  */
/* fail, transaction integrity will be lost           */
if(err3 = (update3, parm31 . . . .))
{
/* put error handling here */
}
.
.
.
```

Since the updates follow closely, the probability of failure has been decreased, but note that if update1 fails and the rest of the updates are completed, then transaction integrity will be lost because the files are now out of sync, or if update1 succeeds and either of the following updates fails, transaction integrity will be lost because the files are out of sync.

Transaction integrity can be maintained in case update1 fails by coding the program so that the other updates do not occur. The program cannot protect against loss of transaction integrity if the first update succeeds and one of the others fails.

4.7   SECURITY CONSIDERATIONS

Security with file servers usually consists of user identification procedures provided by password access to individual servers and individual file protection by user authorization for each file. These provisions can prevent accidental access but become inadequate to protect against willful unauthorized access or harm. (See Chapter 10 for more information on security.)

4.8   ADVANTAGES OF FILE SERVERS

File servers provide a number of advantages over individual unconnected work stations and individual work stations connected in the network:

- The enterprise data is contained in a single place, making access to everyone easier.
- Administrative control of centralized data is easier.
- Storing application source on the server facilitates version control.
- Costs may be lower than using individual work stations because disk storage requirements are lowered.

A common goal is to make the enterprise data generally available to all personnel who require information. File servers can provide a solution. When central control of data becomes essential to provide accurate and meaningful data, then file servers can satisfy this essential need.

If program development is being done at a number of work stations, protection against runaway versions can be provided by file servers. Many small development shops have found that this is sufficient reason to provide a central server to store program source.

4.9   DISADVANTAGES OF FILE SERVERS

The disadvantages of file servers over individual work stations include these:

- Performance degradation due to network transmission.
- Cost of maintaining the network. Maintaining any network adds cost. Maintaining a network that includes a server is certainly no more costly than maintaining any similar network, but if the network is being installed specifically to support a server, then this cost must be considered.
- Exposure to loss of large amounts of data if the server is damaged. Additional exposure to loss of large amounts of data can be incurred when important data is stored essentially in one place. Providing backups becomes important, as does protection of the server. Additional costs are incurred when these problems are addressed.
- Potentially more complex application development. Application development can become more complex, requiring more highly skilled developers. Depending on the needs of the users, complexity can be partially offset by treating all files, including those physically on a server, as if they were local. The downside is that this technique places a higher load on the network and can reduce performance.
- More complex administration. Administration of any network is more complex than stand-alone work stations. A server may decrease the effect of this complexity by allowing easier centralized administration. Network cost must be included when considering adding a server to support a set of stand-alone work stations.

Database Servers

5.1   HOW DATABASE SERVERS WORK

To many people, using a database server is synonymous with client/server; indeed, nearly all products advertised as client/server are based on the database server architecture. It is important to understand that although database servers are a big advance over file servers, they have limitations, especially in their ability to support high performance when there are a large number of simultaneous users.

Database servers use a *data request architecture,* which provides for clients requesting services from servers. Servers in a data request architecture are limited to responding to requests and cannot initiate interaction with clients. Services are allowed to act as clients and request services from other servers.

A *database server* limits the requests for service to retrieving data from the server. Stored procedures capabilities provided by the database are an extension of the database server. Stored procedures can be used to improve the performance characteristics of a database server system.

Figure 5.1 illustrates the flow of information and control in a database server system. The application program contains database access requests, such as SQL statements. During compilation and linking of the program, a remote database access stub,

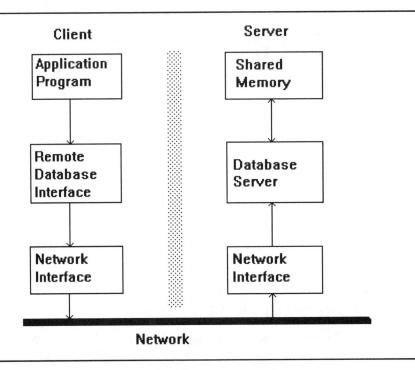

Figure 5.1   Database server architecture.

from the database application library, is hard-linked with the program.

The database provides a remote database interface between the application program and the network. It formats the database access requests for transmittal over the network and passes them to the network interface, which places them on the network.

In the server, the network interface recognizes the message and sends it to the database server, which performs the requested operation and returns the result to the application via the network and the client remote database interface.

5.1.1 How the Application Uses the Data Base

Most database server systems allow the application to use the database on the server exactly as if the database were local. The application uses the database in the following way:

- Establishes use of the database by issuing a CONNECT request.
- Issues database access requests.
- May commit any changes made to the database.
- Issues a disconnect request.

The application identifies the database by name for connection. It application never needs to know the location of the database, since administration tables will establish the physical location using the name.

Database requests can be any legal database statement, such as read (SELECT), add rows (INSERT), update rows (UPDATE), or delete (DELETE). Once the connection is established between the database and the application program, these requests can be issued by the application at any time as long as the user has the authority to issue them.

Transactions are completed using the commit (COMMIT WORK) request. This request is needed only if running in transaction mode and updates (INSERT, UPDATE or DELETE) have been issued by the application.

5.1.2 The Remote Database Interface

The remote database interface formats the database access requests from the application program and passes them to the network interface. The formatting function adds a header to the request containing information to direct the network to the correct database on the correct server platform. The information in the header will include:

- The server address, retrieved from administrative tables.
- The identification of the database server, stored during the connect.
- Information needed by the database server to route the results back to the application.

The remote database interface is also active in establishing the connection with the database server. When the connection is being established, the remote database interface finds the name of the server in the administration tables, retrieves its address, and stores it for the duration of the connection.

On MS-DOS systems, the remote database interface is generally hard-linked to the application. On Windows systems, the interface may be hard-linked but is more often contained in a DLL. On UNIX systems, it may be hard-linked, may be an RPC, or may actually be an active process (the daemon).

5.1.3   The Database Server

The database server (sometimes called the database instantiation):

- Receives database access requests from the network for the application program that has established a particular connection.
- Causes database access requests to be executed by the database.
- Maintains information about previous requests needed to service potential future requests during this connection, called the *context*.

An operating system feature, shared memory, is used to store information, such as locks, that is required for communication among multiple database servers.

Some databases create a new database server process for each connection established; others use a single database server to service many connections. (Reusing a single server to service many connections is called *multithreading*.)

The database server from some vendors is actually the entire set of programs comprising the database system. Other vendors provide a separate process to maintain context, using one or more multithreaded processes for the actual database. In the latter case, the process that maintains the context is called the database server.

5.1.4   Single-Threaded Servers

A server that can process only one connection at a time is called a *single-threaded server*. Figure 5.2 illustrates single-threaded servers.

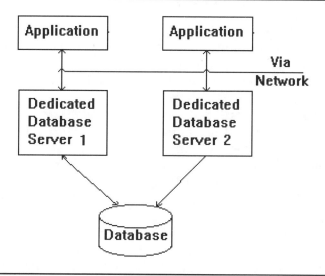

Figure 5.2   Single-threaded servers.

Databases that use the single-threaded architecture assign a server to an application program when it connects. The server remains dedicated to the application until the application disconnects. As additional applications request connection, more servers are started as necessary to service requests.

If there are not too many application programs active with the database at any given time, single-threaded servers will provide high performance because of their simplicity. But as more application programs acquire a server, the system resources become over-loaded with managing multiple processes. Systems designed with single-threaded servers therefore support high performance for a few high-usage application programs. If each application program is written to handle multiple users, a single-threaded database can provide good performance for a reasonable number of users. If the application programs each handle only one user, then the number of users becomes limited.

Single-threaded servers have the advantage of simplicity and were the most common with early data-base products. Few data-bases from major vendors use these servers today.

5.1.5 Multithreaded Dedicated Servers

When the system allows more than one application to connect to a server at the same time and the server is dedicated to serving the connection from each of those applications, the server is called a *multithreaded dedicated server*. Figure 5.3 illustrates multithreaded dedicated servers.

Each multithreaded server can provide service to a number of connected applications at the same time. Once an application has established a connection, it is assigned a specific server which becomes dedicated to serving that application until the connection is completed. Multithreaded servers can take advantage of disk wait time by providing processing for another client. The value of multithreaded servers is limited by the ability of the disk I/O system to handle multiple requests. If the disk system can handle only one I/O request at a time, then the multithreaded server may be blocked once it has reached a point at which each request for service is waiting on a return from the disk. Thus,

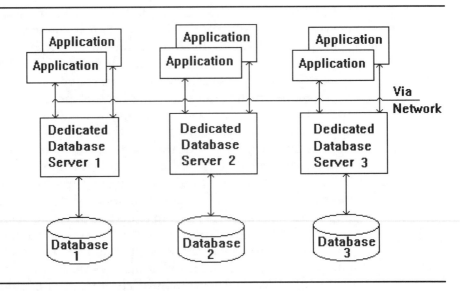

Figure 5.3   Multithreaded dedicated servers.

multithreaded servers often end up essentially single threaded because they are waiting on disk I/O.

Multithreaded servers can improve performance when multiple disk paths are available and the mix of service requests does not cause the server to stop processing (block) while waiting for completion of I/O from a previously received request.

Multithreaded servers are subject to the same locking problem as any other scheme. If the first application begins an update transaction, other applications may be prevented from processing while waiting for the update transaction to complete, because they are attempting to access data locked by the database to protect the integrity of the data.

Multithreaded servers can also improve performance in some environments, notably UNIX, because minimizing the number of processes significantly reduces operating system overhead. In fact, multithreaded servers are important for just this reason.

5.1.6   The Oracle7 Method

Oracle7 improves performance by providing a combination of multithreaded, nondedicated servers and an intelligent buffering technique. Figure 5.4 illustrates the Oracle7 server architecture.

The Oracle7 server system includes a message queue manager, one or more dispatchers, and multithreaded servers. The request from the application is routed by the network listener to a dispatcher, places the request on the request queue. The first server to become available reads a request from the request queue, processes it, and places the result on the response queue. A dispatcher reads the response queue and forwards it to the proper application. The dispatcher will detect when more servers are needed to handle the number of requests and starts additional servers as required.

Oracle7 (as did Oracle version 6) uses a method of storing changes to a redo log as they are made. Writing to the log is much faster than actually placing the changed data into the database. As CPU time and disk channels become available, Oracle7 writes the changes to the database.

Since several Oracle7 multithreaded servers can access the

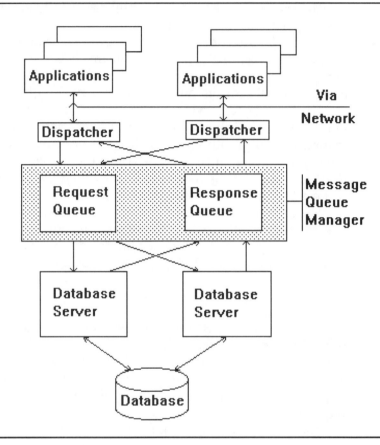

Figure 5.4   Oracle7 server architecture.

same database, server performance is improved to a limit determined by the capabilities of the server hardware rather than by a limit imposed by a blocked database server. The performance of this system is particularly improved when using a parallel computer with an SMP operating system.

5.1.7   Parallel Servers

A new and powerful database capability has recently become available. This feature, called a parallel server, provides the ability to share a large disk array, commonly called a disk farm, among multiple computing platforms. The product from Oracle, Oracle7 Parallel Server, is in use in several locations.

In Figure 5.5, the disk farm is connected to two UNIX platforms, which together act as a single server to the network. Updates made from either server go to the same disk system and are

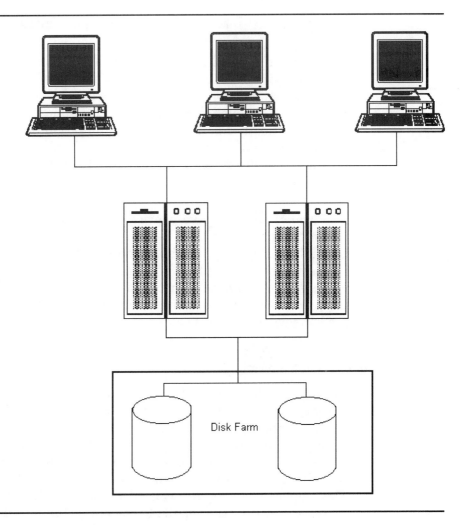

Figure 5.5   Parallel server.

replicated within the disk farm. When transactions are committed, the system ensures that both the primary and secondary location have been updated. The database software ensures that the multiple platforms do not conflict by managing locking mechanisms that are shared by all platforms connected with the disk farm. Although the diagram shows two servers, more can be attached to provide the computing power required to support the enterprise.

The parallel server has the following advantages:

- Improved scalability, since more computing power can be added without changing any software.
- Improved failover over other types of schemes.
- Failover completely transparent to applications, since it is automatically handled by the combination of hardware and software.
- Improved system availability, since there is no single point of failure.

Parallel servers have a price as well: loss of performance. Locking mechanisms must be maintained on disk, requiring additional I/O for every database access. This loss of performance has been measured as high as 25 percent when compared to running a single platform without using the parallel server feature. Improvements are being made, and future versions and newer products will reduce this cost.

5.1.8   Sybase Open Server

Sybase provides a multithreaded database server similar in operation to the Oracle7 method. Sybase also provides an additional capability with its Open Server, which supports executing an application program that can receive requests from the client for servicing. The Open Server application program can then access the database in the same manner as any other program. This application program can do whatever calculations are required and return the results to the requester. The designer can reduce network load and improve the performance of the system. The Sybase Open Server provides many of the characteristics of enhanced client/server described in Chapter 7.

5.2 DISTRIBUTED DATA TECHNOLOGY

5.2.1 Definition of a Distributed Database

In order to provide computing services for people in workplaces at dispersed geographic locations, it is necessary to provide data in local storage for improved performance. The local data is thus available for the moment-to-moment work of users at that location. Centralized data remains necessary for storing information critical to the whole enterprise. Sometimes people at one location require data stored in another local storage. Distributed databases provide the capability to access data from any location, no matter where it is actually stored.

Data required to support the operation of the enterprise that is stored in more than one physical (or logical) location is known as *distributed data,* and the software used to provide access to distributed data is called a *distributed database* (Figure 5.6) Distributed databases use a *two-phase commit* protocol to maintain data integrity. (Appendix D explains how two-phase commit operates.)

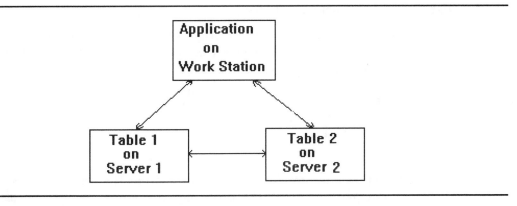

Figure 5.6   Distributed database.

5.2.2 Functionality in a Distributed Database

A distributed database will always provide:

- The capability to manage physically dispersed data as if it were a single database.
- The ability to present the information in the database to the application as if all the data were in one location.
- Protection against failure during update transactions by use of a two-phase commit protocol or equivalent.

A distributed database may also provide one or more of the following capabilities:

- Maintenance of redundant physical storage of all or selected parts of the data (replication).
- Ability to substitute a part of the redundant data automatically in the case of failure of a portion of the system (failover).
- Ability to remain operational 24 hours a day, seven days a week (24 × 7 operation).
- Capability to modify limited portions of the database definitions without shutting the system down.
- Ability to break a table into parts and store them at different locations yet present the table as a single entity (partitioning).

5.2.3 Distributed Database Access

Figure 5.6 illustrates a distributed database at a high level. Using a relational database as an example, suppose the application uses the following SQL statement to access data:

```
SELECT *
    FROM TABLE1, TABLE2
    WHERE
        TABLE1KEY = TABLE2KEY;
```

This statement retrieves all the data from the database where the key in a row in TABLE1 equals the key in a row in TABLE2. This operation creates a *join* of TABLE1 and TABLE2. The statement is executed by the database system and the results returned such that the distribution of the data over two physical locations is not apparent to the application. The application connects to the database and issues requests for access as if the database were located in a single place.

5.2.4 Joins

When data is required from two or more tables to satisfy the application request, it is called a join. An example is the SQL statement:

```
SELECT *
    FROM TABLE1, TABLE2
    WHERE
        TABLE1KEY = TABLE2KEY;
```

The database software logically breaks the join into two statements:*

```
SELECT *
    FROM TABLE1;
```

and

```
SELECT *
    FROM TABLE2;
```

As the software retrieves each row from the tables, it compares the keys and returns the rows with equal keys to the application.

There are two ways for the database system to satisfy the requirements of the statement. In the first case, the database software on the work station retrieves data from both TABLE1 and TABLE2 by accessing the individual servers. The resources of the work station are used to do the join, and all access to data is via the network. In the second case, the work station is connected to Server 1. The database software in Server 1 retrieves data

---

*This is a simplistic view of what actually happens. The mathematically correct discussion would take much more space and would impart no useful additional information.

from TABLE1 locally and TABLE2 via the network. Only the results are placed on the network to return to the work station. Database products will always have a system to optimize joins.

Consider the situation whereby TABLE1 has only a few rows but TABLE2 has more than a million. If the system accesses all the rows from TABLE2 to merge them with TABLE1, there will be a large amount of traffic on the network, and the join will take a long time. If the system detects that there are only a few rows in TABLE1 and retrieves them first, using the data in these rows to search the rows in TABLE2, only the rows of TABLE2 required to satisfy the request will be returned from Server 2.

Optimizing joins and other complex searches of the database is a difficult issue. It has been amply studied, and most modern databases include very good optimizing methods.Nevertheless, no matter how efficient the optimizing is, a join over the network will put a lot of traffic on the network. For this reason, it is a good idea not to attempt complex joins, or if possible, no joins, over the network.

Joins can occur when the user is not aware that one is actually happening. For instance, if the database is performing referential integrity checking (making sure the master is there before the data), the system must, in effect, join the table being checked with the referenced table (the master). If this feature of the database is being used, it is vital that all the tables involved with a given referential check be on the same physical server.

5.2.5   The Distributed Data Dictionary

Database software must have information about the database, such as which columns are in what tables and where those tables are located. The part of the database that provides this information is called the *data dictionary*. The data dictionary is a set of tables stored in the database itself and accessed by the database software in much the same way as the user data is accessed. The data dictionary can be considered as an application designed and used by the database software for its work.

If the database is all in one place, the data dictionary is always available to the server for every request. If the database is distributed, then a *distributed data dictionary* becomes necessary. For instance, if Server 1 is attempting to access data that is not resident on it, the software must have access to the information required to determine the actual location of the table it is trying to access.

When the database is started, a data dictionary containing all the information about the entire database, including its physical location, can be built within every platform required for efficient access. As long as there are no changes to the data dictionary, this system works well. But there are two situations which can create difficulties for a distributed data dictionary.

First, if there are changes to the definitions of the tables within the database, such as adding new tables or changing the column definitions, there must be a way of updating the data dictionary dynamically. As long as these types of changes are few, the temporary loss of availability during the data dictionary update will not cause a noticeable problem. Good database management can therefore prevent this problem from becoming severe.

Databases store statistical information about the tables in the data dictionary for use by the optimizer. Some vendors include the capability to maintain this information dynamically. This method makes the optimizer a great deal more efficient, but if the database is distributed, the cost of updating the data dictionary at many locations can become a problem. These systems will include ways to overcome this problem partially, and the database administrator (DBA) should be aware of how to customize the system.

If there is a lot of update activity (UPDATE, DELETE, INSERT), then the optimization system can be severely affected by the data in the database. Some databases, such as DB2, do not dynamically update statistical information. DB2 optimizes when the SQL statements in the application are compiled (the operation called *bind*) using statistics created by a utility. The statistics utility is executed by the DBA periodically. If there is a lot of activity and the database is distributed, a static set of statistics can become a problem as the optimizer continues to act using obsolete information.

If a distributed data dictionary becomes large because there are a lot of tables with many columns, then storing the data dictionary on many platforms can become a problem because of the amount of storage required at each platform and the time it takes to move the data dictionary at start-up. Again, a user considering a distributed database must take into account the implications of the distributed data dictionary as well as the distribution of user data.

5.3   APPLICATION DESIGN CONSIDERATIONS

5.3.1   Single Server Considerations

Any design of a database client/server system using a single server must include the following considerations:

- The number of users who will be connected to the database at any given time
- Frequency of access by those signed on
- Power of the server
- Complexity of database access
- Bandwidth of the network
- Difference between peak load and normal load
- Willingness to accept degraded response times during peak load

If the number of planned simultaneous users is small—around ten* or fewer—there is no need to do anything more than install and run the system. As the number of users begins to rise, the need to design the system carefully and use available tools becomes exponentially more important. Somewhere around 20 users, it becomes necessary to examine all factors and maximize the efficiency of the system. Using a single server, no matter how powerful, and any database product can produce some unpleasant performance surprises if the system is not carefully designed.

Even if a number of users are connected to the database, they do not present a problem if they make infrequent use of the database. Analyzing this factor can be difficult, since it depends on

---

*These numbers can vary by orders of magnitude, depending on the hardware and software used, as well as the application. These are based on the author's experience with MS-DOS and Windows systems. Generally, UNIX systems are more powerful and the numbers very different.

the application, the tendency of users to sign on and then leave the system without using it, and so forth. The analyst must examine how users will use the system before this factor becomes important.

The power of the server platform is important in determining the expected performance of the system. If the server has sufficient power, it will not be a bottleneck to performance. Determining the power of the server includes defining its CPU power, considering whether it is a parallel machine, and measuring disk I/O capability. In addition, the availability of multiple disk drives must be considered. Multiple disk drives allow table spaces to be spread over multiple physical disks to reduce head movement and provide capability for parallel disk access. The speed and number of the disk channels must also be considered.

Complex database access can put a heavy load on the server. When requests to the database include compound SELECTs, complex joins of more than two tables, updates or deletes that affect multiple rows, or large found sets, then access is considered complex. (The found set includes all the rows that meet the matching criteria stated in the SELECT.) If these conditions exist, the database server is loaded much more heavily by each user than otherwise. Performance degradation because of complex access can be overcome to a great extent by increasing the power of the server.

In many cases, the bandwidth of the network is the determining factor for system performance when using a database server. If all the application processing is happening in the work station, then all data and the access to the database is being transferred over the network. Since each transaction will probably require multiple accesses to the database to retrieve multiple rows of data, the load on the network to update the database can become very high. While the server is relieving the network of the traffic for disk I/O, a lot of traffic will still be generated by the multiple accesses to the database to acquire the data necessary for the processing. Many users have been disappointed in performance of the database server due to network bottlenecks. Perhaps the most important factor in designing the system is to ensure that the network is capable of handling the traffic necessary to provide required performance.

Defining required performance must include consideration of the average load and the peak load. The following questions must be answered:

- What is the desired response time?
- Will the peak load be considerably higher than the average load?
- Is it satisfactory to accept longer response times during peak loads?
- Is the peak load frequent or infrequent?

5.3.2 Multiple Servers and Distributed Databases

Designs for multiple server and distributed databases must consider all the points mentioned for single server systems. In addition, they must also consider:

- Using a distributed database
- Frequency of using joins
- Horizontally partitioned data (one table spread over two locations)
- Data location (table location)
- Frequency of access to each table
- Requirement for the application to access both local and remote information

The existence of multiple servers on the network does not always imply that the system must use a distributed database. Consideration should always be given to putting the complete database for each application on a single server. Unless this introduces a bottleneck to performance, keeping away from distributed database overhead always produces better performance and easier administration.

The nature of joins dictates that, for each join, all the tables in the join should be on the same server. This rule can be broken only if the join that spans servers will be used rarely. Otherwise, performance inevitably will be poor—not only for the application using the join but perhaps for all applications because of the load the join places on the network.

Horizontally partitioned databases present a particularly tricky problem to existing database systems. Suppose that the enterprise would like to have the corporate customer list broken up so that each branch office can access its own customers locally. The enterprise also needs to have the entire customer list available from any location, especially from headquarters. This situation illustrates a horizontally partitioned database. Consider a statement such as:

```
SELECT *
    FROM CUSTOMER_TABLE
    WHERE
        CUSTOMER_LAST_PURCHASE > 01/01/92;
```

If the database supports horizontally partitioned data, this statement will cause the database to search the entire customer table at all locations in the enterprise. Few, if any, major database vendors support this type of partitioning well.

Horizontal partitioning can be replaced by program knowledge that there are multiple databases and searching each one individually. To do this, the program must have access to a list of the individual tables that make up the true customer table.

In spite of its apparent difficulties, horizontal partitioning can be effective in making information more immediately available at the point it is used most frequently. Horizontal partitioning is one of the major tools that allow a system design to take advantage of distributed databases.

From a design perspective, there are three possible locations for any table: on the work station in use, on a local server, or on a remote server.

Tables on the work stations have extremely limited use in most enterprises and may not be possible because the work stations are diskless. One rare case in which a table on the work station may be useful is for data that is used by only a single user who is the usual user of the work station. This might be the case when a single person is assigned to manage data that is not generally required by the rest of the enterprise.

Tables on local servers may be at the heart of the system. Most of the data accessed at a branch office will be on a local server. Since LANs are generally faster than WANs, distributed systems should be designed to use local tables as much as possible and still provide the required functionality.

Tables at central points are often accessed by WAN from remote sites. Also, tables that are local at a branch office may be accessed from other branch offices via WAN. The system must be designed to make access from the branch offices to central tables minimal.

5.3.3   Application Program Residence

Most development tools available for use with databases do not provide much control over application program residence. In just about every case, the application will run on the work station, using the database interface for data access. Even using C or other such language, placing application programs anywhere but on the work station will definitely increase the complexity of the system and the cost of development.

Since the application is running on the work station, the system should be designed to minimize database access. This is true for any environment but becomes even more important when the network is involved. Each access to the database requires that the access request and supporting information be placed on the network; then the resultant rows must be fetched back over the network. This process usually limits the performance of distributed database applications because of the network load.

5.3.4   Network Load

Database servers are well known for generating a heavy load on the network. Though the network load for database servers is considerably less than for file servers, given the same application, it is still a significant part of performance considerations.

Database servers reduce the network load when compared with file servers because the work of searching the database is in the server rather than in the application. An application may be required to make as many as ten times the use of the network using a file server as using a database server.

Still, the database server is only a place to store data. If the application requires relatively few but complex events, then the database server will work well If the application requires many (simple or complex) accesses to the database, network activity can rise considerably. If there are a number of users, the network can easily become the bottleneck to performance. Great care must be used in designing multiple-user, heavy-access systems using database servers.

5.3.5 Development Tools

The big strength of currently available database products is the large number of excellent development tools available. Most database products provide powerful tools, such as Oracle's SQL*Forms, SQL*Report, and Oracle Card, etc. There are also third-party tools available. All of these tools provide an excellent means for developing simple and complex applications. Many of these tools enable end users to develop ad hoc applications as needed without lengthy training.

5.3.6 Stored Procedures

Some database vendors provide a programming language for writing application procedures that are stored within the database. These procedures, called *stored procedures,* are an important development for the database server environment, especially for distributed database systems, because they provide a means to move parts of the application calculations to the server.

A stored procedure is written as an extension to the database access methods. It is possible to write complex SQL statements with additional tests and calculations so that fairly large subroutines can be included. A stored procedure is invoked from the application program with a single database access call and returns only the result.

Judicious use of stored procedures can decrease the problem of network traffic by moving part of the application to the server. Database vendors that supply this feature provide a means to coordinate stored procedures with the development tools used to write the work station application.

Generally personnel require training before being able to use stored procedures effectively. The system designer must be aware of the capabilities of stored procedures, how they are invoked from the application, and how they affect the internal performance of the database.

5.3.7   Stored Procedures with Oracle

Oracle stored procedures (named *stored subprograms* by Oracle) are created with a proprietary language from Oracle called PL/SQL. PL/SQL may be used both for creating stored subprograms and as an embedded extended SQL within a program written in C or COBOL. Stored subprograms may be invoked from C or COBOL with a special embedded SQL statement:

```
EXEC SQL EXECUTE
    BEGIN
                stored_subprogram_name(:host_
                variable1, ... :host_variablen);
    END;
END-EXEC;
```

Stored subprograms can also be invoked from any Oracle tool such as SQL*FORMS in a similar manner.

A stored subprogram example might be:

```
PROCEDURE getcust_name (custno INTEGER, custname
CHAR(30), error_code) IS
BEGIN
    SELECT CUSTNAME INTO custname
        FROM CUSTTABLE
        WHERE CUSTNO = custno;
EXCEPTION
WHEN NO_DATA_FOUND THEN error_code = +100;
WHEN OTHERS THEN error_code = SQLCODE;
END getcust_name;
```

When invoked, this stored subprogram will return the name of the customer for the customer number passed by the calling program.

Oracle PL/SQL provides a nearly complete processing language, and stored subprograms can be used to cause application processing to occur on the server saving considerable network traffic.

5.4 DEVELOPMENT AND END USER TOOLS AVAILABLE

5.4.1 Application Development Tools

Although 3GL languages generate the most efficient systems for client/server applications, increased programmer productivity and decreased maintenance costs are leading many organizations to use 4GL tools. Some 4GLs are designed to maximize the use of specific client platforms. Others can work on multiple platforms but often sacrifice functionality and performance to their goal of portability.

Traditional DOS client/server tools are still regarded as more reliable than their Windows counterparts. RDBMS vendors offer tightly integrated tools designed to make use of an RDBMS' specific capabilities. These were designed to run on dumb terminals as well as PCs and have a long history of use. But since they were designed for dumb terminals, they may not be able to make use of advanced PC or graphical user interface (GUI) capabilities. Neither are they portable between various RDBMSs. Some of these tightly integrated tools are Oracle SQL*Forms, Ingres 4GL, and Windows 4GL, Informix 4GL and Sybase APT Workbench.

Two common portable DOS development tools are DataEase and Borland's Paradox. Both support several database servers, including Microsoft/Sybase SQL Server, Oracle, IBM DB2/2, and MVS DB2—by way of MicroDecisionware's Database gateway product. Paradox will also support DEC's Rdb/VMS.

Since Database has a more transparent link to the back-end database servers, developers are shielded from some of the complexities of client/server development. But to achieve this goal, Database has sacrificed some functionality, so some applications end up being too complex to write in Database.

QBE, Paradox's Query-By-Example, provides a query and reporting tool for developers or endusers. SQL commands are generated automatically and routed to the target database server. Then the results are stored in local answer sets, where they are available for further review and manipulation. Paradox SQL-link is more complex to use, and programmers need knowledge of Paradox's PAL language and the database server's applications programming interface (API) before using this product. But because Paradox first stores database results in a temporary table, which it builds dynamically before any program can operate on the data, it lacks good performance characteristics for applications development.

Plenty of Windows applications development tools are available for client/server processing. All offer basic screen painters that allow programmers to define screen objects such as list boxes, menus, and push buttons, plus a proprietary language in which to build application logic. None is easy to master, each having a three to six months' learning curve.

A few of the most popular tools are SQLWindows, Power-Builder, Visual Basic, and ObjectView. SQLWindows offers a functional programming language plus Quest, a companion query/report-writing tool for endusers. PowerBuilder offers Data-Windows, which allows programmers to design simple screens quickly to access relational tables. ObjectView is capable of running under OS/2 v2.0 as well as Windows, and with ObjectView, developers can build spreadsheet and business graphics into their applications by using its specialized GUI objects.

Uniface is widely used for Oracle and Sybase application development by customers who deploy applications on a wide variety of platforms. It can run on dumb terminals or as a Windows, DOS, OS/2, Open Look, or Motif application. Its architecture allows the developer to describe the application's database structure and business rules into Uniface's data dictionary. Then Uniface can build complex screen objects with a minimum amount of further programming.

Popular tools for the Macintosh are Fourth Dimension and Omnis 7 (which also runs under Windows). Both products can connect to UNIX SQL database servers, and both support Apple's Data Access Language (DAL) language. This allows them to connect up remote relational databases running on minis or mainframes.

One database server for client/server application development, the SQL Server for OS2, is marketed by Microsoft. Another, the SQL Server for UNIX and VAX platforms, is marketed by Sybase.

Sybase, an RDBMS vendor, incorporates client/server capabilities, such as stored procedures and triggers, into its RDBMS engine. Its Open Server architecture allows users to build their own customized application servers. Open Server applications can audit user activity, monitor real-time applications, route messages to remote servers, and access or update non-Sybase files and databases. It can even access legacy data, such as IMS or DB2 databases. The popular Sybase is also supported by many third-party application development and decision support tools.

5.4.2   Interoperability Tools

The barriers to SQL interoperability may be breached by applications programming interfaces (APIs), often called middleware. which provide connectivity between applications and databases.

ODBC is Microsoft's Open Database Connectivity. It will allow Windows-based clients access to data from multiple heterogeneous RDBMSs, such as IBM's DB2, DEC's Rdb, and its own SQL Server. ODBC also links to Apple's DAL, a connectivity language that gives the Macintosh access to servers and host computers, whereas third-party developers like Pioneer Software will address the issue of linking IBM's OS/2 or the myriad UNIX offerings.

IDAPI (Integrated Database Applications Programming Interface initiative) is being marketed by Microsoft's competitors: Borland, IBM, Novell, and WordPerfect. IDAPI, which addresses heterogeneous operating systems, can be implemented once at the server, whereas ODBC is client dependent, requiring multiple updates of remote LANS.

Oracle Corp. has plans to use its Glue software to provide universal access to databases, E-mail, file servers, and personal digital assistants (PDAs). The first release of a Glue development kit is for use on Windows clients.

5.5   DATABASE CAPACITY

For many situations, the capacity of a database product is of little importance, since products from major vendors can manage databases of hundreds of gigabytes. Though the number of bytes that can be managed is large, the number of rows in a single table may be severely limited—often at 10 million rows—a limitation that can cause severe database design difficulties.

Before installing a database product, every enterprise should check the capacity of the database to manage data against the specific need. Some of the capacity limits that appear are these:

- Total number of bytes which can be managed in a single database.
- Total number of bytes that can be managed in a single table.
- Total number of rows allowed in a single table.
- Number of indexes allowed in a database and for a table.
- Number of tables allowed in a database.

5.6 DATABASE ADMINISTRATION IN THE CLIENT/SERVER ENVIRONMENT

5.6.1 Database and Table Location

Intelligent database and table location are critical to success of client/server systems. The following can be done:

- Place tables as close as possible to the location of most frequent usage.
- Put sets of tables on different disk drives (database spans multiple disks).
- If more than one LAN connection is available to work stations, frequently used tables should be spread among available LAN connections.

Whenever possible, tables should be as close as possible to the location where they are most frequently used to minimize the use of slower WAN networks. "Close" is defined here in network terms—that is, if the database is attached to a single hop on a LAN from the work station, it is as close as possible. A database on a WAN is as far as possible. Frequently used tables should have the fastest possible access, and WANs are generally slower than LANs, so performance can be badly affected if tables are frequently accessed via a WAN.

Tables should be spread among multiple disks on the same

server if possible. Most databases allow this approach by use of *database spanning* (sometimes called *tablespace spanning*). If tables are on different disk drives, disk head movement is minimized, increasing performance considerably.

If multiple LANs are available from the work stations, the databases should be spread among them. Applications using database servers place a very heavy load on networks. Spreading access among multiple LANs can increase performance by decreasing the load on the individual subnetworks. If this method is combined with keeping access on single hop LANs, performance can be made much faster than otherwise.

5.6.2   Defining Database Access and Security

Database servers require careful consideration of who gets access to the various databases and tables located on the server. Since effective server use requires that many people have access to the server and network security limits server access, database and individual table access is the only standard method that can limit access to the database.

Database products require that individuals sign on to each database in use. Relational databases also provide a *GRANT privileges* feature to control access of individual tables. The administrator must be fully knowledgeable of these techniques and use them to allow easy access by authorized users and prevent access by those not authorized. Since the server may be supporting a mission-critical system, database access in a client/server system requires careful thought and execution. (See Chapter 10 for more information on security.)

5.6.3   Physical Location of Applications and Tools

In general, there is little choice of where applications are executed when using database servers. All known tools for use with databases require the application to execute on the work station. The only choice is where the application is stored. If the application is generally completely loaded and does not require continued access to application executables, then the physical location of the application executable is not quite as important, and it may be advantageous to store a single copy of the application on a server.

Most modern application development tools generate executables that require continuous loading of modules from disk storage. In this case, performance and network load considerations require storing the application on the work station. Performance can be dramatically affected when the application is stored on a server supporting a database via the same LAN. If diskless work stations are used, the only solution is to access the application over a different LAN from the database access, unless the network has an extremely high bandwidth or there are few simultaneous users.

Applications developed with some tools require that at least some portion of the tool (the *operational environment*) be executed during application execution. In these cases, the operational environment must be stored in the same location as the application itself. Since some vendors charge for each copy of the operational environment, costs can rise unexpectedly.

Location of development tools is less critical because the performance requirements during development are generally not as stringent as for production systems. If development personnel are using a different network from production, this becomes even less important, and the use of diskless work stations for development becomes quite practical.

5.7   ADVANTAGES OF DATABASE SERVERS

When making any comparisons, the objects being compared must be defined before implications of the comparison can be understood. In the client/server environment, we want to compare what we are contemplating to something we already know about. Most of the advantages of database servers are those that make the database server more useful than either a file server or the monolithic mainframe. The advantages listed here address this comparison.

The primary advantages of the database server result in improved performance per dollar over the mainframe and improved performance and decreased development cost over the file server. Other advantages include ease of use by the end user, easier administration due to centralized databases, and improved ability to scale the system to the needs of the enterprise. These advantages are the result of several features:

- Searches happen in the server, freeing the work station to do end user interfaces.
- Data resides in one known place and is easier to access from many locations.
- Development and maintenance of applications is less costly and faster because of the large number of tools available.
- Database vendors provide a number of mature systems to work with.
- There are a large number of application packages available for use with database servers.

5.8 DISADVANTAGES OF DATABASE SERVERS

The disadvantages of database servers can best be discussed as costs associated with gaining the advantages of these servers. But in many cases, these disadvantages can be overcome by using enhanced client/server products and techniques. The disadvantages mentioned here are made in comparison with monolithic mainframes, file servers, and enhanced client/server:

- Database servers place a very heavy load on the network, causing either failure to perform or greatly increased cost.
- There is no reasonable way to balance the load among servers and/or work stations once the system is built.
- There are increased security exposures when compared to the mainframe.
- Data distribution remains difficult to manage when compared with enhanced client/server.

6

A Sample Database Server Application

This chapter will describe an order entry system developed using a database server. The system requirements are described in Appendix A and the network architecture is in Appendix B. In order to meet the requirements for the system, certain compromises will be made. Compromises should be considered as a means to accommodate the real world as closely as possible to the desired results.

The sample system described here designed is designed to show the characteristics of database servers. It is not necessarily a complete system but will illustrate what is necessary to make functional systems in the client/server environment when only database servers are used.

6.1 THE DATABASE

6.1.1 Data Requirements

The database will consist of the following tables:

- Customer (containing customer addresses, special discount information, etc.)
- Inventory master (containing product description, price information, etc.)

- Warehouse stock levels (containing the inventory levels for each warehouse)
- Accounts receivable (containing the customer aged balances)
- Order header (containing the customer number, the order status, the shipping address for this order, the customer purchase order number and other miscellaneous information common to the entire order)
- Order detail (containing the item number, the quantity ordered, the price per item, discount given, etc.)

6.1.2 Database Definitions

The customer table was created with the following SQL statement:

```
CREATE TABLE CUSTOMER
      UNIQUE CUSTNO CHAR(8) NOT NULL,
      CUSTNAME CHAR(35),
      CUSTADD1 CHAR(35),
      CUSTADD2 CHAR(35),
      CUSTADD3 CHAR(35),
      CUSTADD4 CHAR(35),
      CUSTCITY CHAR(25),
      CUSTZIP CHAR(10),
      CUSTDISC CHAR(1),
      CUSTDPER NUMERIC(4,2);
```

The inventory table was created with this statement:

```
CREATE TABLE INVENTORY
      UNIQUE INVNUM CHAR(12) NOT NULL,
      INVNAM CHAR(15),
      INVBPRCE NUMERIC(3,6),
      INVDCD1 CHAR(1),
      INVDQTY1 INTEGER,
      INVDPER1 NUMERIC(4,2),
      INVDCD2 CHAR(1),
      INVDQTY2 INTEGER,
      INVDPER2 NUMERIC(4,2),
      INVDCD3 CHAR(1),
      INVDQTY3 INTEGER,
      INVDPER3 NUMERIC(4,2);
```

The warehouse stock level table was created with this statement:

```
CREATE TABLE STKLEV
    UNIQUE WREHSE CHAR(4) NOT NULL,
    WRESTKNUM CHAR(15),
    WRELEV INTEGER;
```

The order header table was created with this statement:

```
CREATE TABLE ORDHEAD
    UNIQUE ORDNUM CHAR(7) NOT NULL,
    ORDCUST CHAR(8),
    ORDCPO CHAR(20),
    ORDEDATE DATE,
    CUSTNAME CHAR(35),
    ORDSADD1 CHAR(35),
    ORDSADD2 CHAR(35),
    ORDSADD3 CHAR(35),
    ORDSADD4 CHAR(35),
    ORDSCITY CHAR(25),
    ORDSZIP CHAR(10),
    ORDSTAT CHAR(1);
```

The first two characters of the order number will be the office code: the rest of the number will be assigned sequentially by the system.

The order line item table was created with this statement:

```
CREATE TABLE ORDLINE
    UNIQUE LINONUM CHAR(7) NOT NULL,
    LINNO INTEGER,
    LINITEM CHAR(12),
    LINQTY INTEGER,
    LINDCD CHAR(1),
    LINDPER NUMERIC(4,2),
    LINSTAT CHAR(1),
    LINWRE CHAR(4);
```

The accounts receivable table is defined by the accounts receivable system. The aged balance and credit code will be used by the order entry system to determine the creditworthiness of the customer.

6.1.3   System Design Considerations

The database will be designed using the following assumptions:

- A 10 Mb LAN.
- A 56 Kb WAN.
- There is sufficient computing power in the servers and work stations to make the network the deciding factor.
- Average, or normal, usage is by 30 simultaneous users.
- The system must be designed to handle three orders per second, and allow for short peak loads up to five orders per second.
- The average order has ten line items.
- Each SQL statement from the work station is 100 bytes long, including necessary control information.
- Each SQL statement returns 100 bytes of data, including necessary control information, with the exception that retrieval of customer information, requires 200 bytes of data returned.
- The average order requires one access to the customer master, ten accesses to inventory, one access to accounts receivable, one access to the order header, and five accesses to the order detail, for a total of 18 database requests.
- The work stations will have sufficient disk to hold database vendor tools and the developed applications.

Development cost will be kept low by using the database vendor's tools. These tools will cause all application execution to take place in the work station.

6.1.4   The System Design

Design Attempt 1   The first design attempt will be to use the simplest approach. It will have the following characteristics:

- All databases will be on the central storage at the home office.
- The databases will be accessed via the WAN.
- All development will be done using the database vendor 4GL.
- When orders are complete, the best warehouse to ship from will be determined by the programs in the work station and the order sent to that warehouse.

Using these assumptions, the average order will require the following database access:

- One SELECT access each to the customer master, the accounts receivable, and the order header tables.
- Ten SELECT accesses to the inventory master.
- One OPEN cursor and up to four FETCHs from the warehouse stock table for each inventory retrieval.

The message that sends the SELECT, OPEN, and FETCH statement to the central server is about 100 bytes long, including control information. Assume that the return message from the database is 100 bytes for each database, except that the message from the customer master is 200 bytes. Adding up the bytes transmitted in both directions for data retrieval for each order, we get 10,700 bytes. Updates require another 300 bytes, or about 11,000 bytes per order. At three orders per second, this implies a load of 264,000 bits per second for this design approach—a result way beyond the capacity of the WAN. The designers will need to find another approach.

Design Attempt 2 After much calculation, including peak loads and the need to transfer completed orders to a warehouse, the designers came up with the following design approach:

- The inventory master will be maintained on the central server at the home office.
- The accounts receivable and the customer master will be downloaded each night to the branch office servers.
- Updates to the customer master will be logged at each branch and transmitted to the home office each night, where a local application will update the customer master before downloading begins.
- The inventory on-hand quantity will be updated as each order is completed, using a stored procedure in the central server.
- The item name and discounts allowable will be downloaded to the branch offices each night for reference during order entry.
- Orders will be sent to the warehouses from the work stations during the day as they are completed.
- The order tables will be sent to the home office each night.

This approach results in something less than the company wants but will work. It will require 24-hour access to the WAN so that the interchange of information can occur during the night.

The calculations are:

- Accesses to the local servers for the customer master and the order tables will not load the LANs appreciably.
- Since inventory updating and accounts receivable checking will be done by a stored procedure, only a single message need be sent on the WAN with a short reply, each request message will be about 50 bytes, and each response will be about 200 bytes per order.
- The decision to complete the order will be made in the stored procedure so that the updating can take place without another database access from the work stations.
- Orders transmitted to the warehouse will require 450 bytes of data per order on the average.

The total load on the 56 Kb WAN will be 15,600 bits per second during off-peak and 26,000 during peak hours. Both figures will allow for other activity and for instantaneous high peaks. Also, the load will leave room for additional capacity and allow using the WAN for other purposes uses during the day.

Besides not quite meeting the requirements, this approach will require that part of the development is done in the more complex and harder-to-master language provided by the database vendor for stored procedures, but the design team believes that this is the best compromise for the circumstances.

Alternatives Considered A number of alternatives were considered and rejected before deciding on Design Attempt2:

- Maintain all databases at the home office and use stored procedures exclusively. Rejected because of the programming complexity and doubt that the human interface could be properly controlled. Also, modifications would become expensive.
- Use software in the work stations to make them into "dumb"

terminals, creating and placing the application exclusively on the central server. Rejected because of plans to use the branch office work stations as ad hoc query stations and other expansion plans.

- Other combinations of database deployment. Rejected because of complexity of administration and control using the tools available with the database.

6.2   HOW THE SYSTEM WILL WORK

For new orders, applications running on work stations (created with database tools) will:

- Interface with users, presenting information and accepting input.
- Access the local customer master for customer information.
- Access the local partial inventory master to retrieve the item name and the discount rules.
- When the order has been completely entered, invoke the stored procedures at the home office central server to complete the order.
- Update the order header and order detail tables with order information.
- When an order is completed, select the warehouse or warehouses to send the order to and transmit it.

Stored procedures at the central server will:

- Examine the accounts receivable table to determine the customer creditworthiness.
- Examine the inventory tables to determine which warehouse has sufficient stock for each item.
- If all items are available and the customer credit check is proper, decrease the stock level of a warehouse and indicate the warehouse to ship each item from.
- Return a message to the work station indicating the status of each check.

Queries about stock levels and so forth will operate in a similar way. Queries about order status will first examine the local order tables and if the order is not found there examine the central order tables. All queries will run on the work stations, sending queries to the central server as necessary. The anticipated load of order entry plus the relatively small number of queries are not expected to overload the WAN.

Enhanced Client/Server Processing

7.1 ENHANCED CLIENT/SERVER BASICS

7.1.1 Characteristics of Enhanced Client/Server

Enhanced client/server systems are separate from the database system and therefore can be used to manage the client/server environment in the most efficient manner possible. Enhanced client/server systems, cooperating with database server products to provide extended capabilities, are a natural environment in which application processes can be modularized into client programs and server programs that can be distributed about the network efficiently.

The enhanced client/server model is shown in Figure 7.1. In this architecture, clients request services by name, and the system routes the request to the named service. When the service has completed its work, it returns the result to the client by simply using a return function. Neither the client nor the server requires information on the location of the other. The server application programs may reside on any platform in the system and may be moved administratively for improved efficiency without programming involvement.

Enhanced client/server technology is provided by separate software from databases or file servers. On the theory that man-

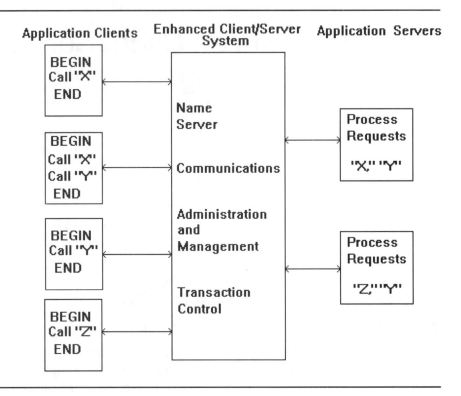

Figure 7.1 Enhanced client/server architecture.

aging client/server and/or fully distributed resources cannot be easily mingled with database management, vendors have created software that concentrates on managing the client/server environment. In general, enhanced client/server software provides the following services:

- Two-phase commit management among many *resource managers*. (Resource managers are discussed more fully later; for now they can be considered simply as databases).
- Automatic routing of service requests to the appropriate application server.
- Routing based on the contents of the message being sent with the request, called *data-dependent routing*.

- Automatic load balancing among multiple application servers assigned the same task.
- Rerouting in the case of partial system failure.
- Automatic restart of servers when a server fails.
- Migrating servers and/or groups of servers to an alternate platform in the case of partial system failure.

All of the features can be controlled administratively while the system is running and do not in any way affect the application programming. Enhanced client/server technology allows programming and system design techniques that dramatically reduce the network load and reduce the costs of moving data from one server to another or totally reconfiguring the network.

7.1.2   OLTP and Enhanced Client/Server

On-line transaction processing (OLTP) has been used for many years to describe a specific type of computer usage. No real definition has ever been devised, but it is generally agreed that OLTP is characterized by:

- Rapid, interactive interfaces with users
- Support for mission-critical applications
- Transaction-oriented processing
- Support for a large number of users

As OLTP systems were developed to support fully distributed computing on open systems platforms, application developers discovered that these systems did more than provide OLTP capabilities. Managers and developers also discovered that, in fact, all production applications processed transactions. Once these discoveries were made, people involved with distributed computing realized that the modern OLTP system provides something beyond simple client/server and OLTP—hence, the designation enhanced client/server.

7.1.3   Typical Platforms

Modern enhanced client/server systems provide support for a wide range of platforms, including use of almost any UNIX-based server and MS-DOS, OS/2, and UNIX work stations. These systems have been ported in some cases to a number of proprietary platforms such as VMS, but the demand has not been sufficient to keep these ports up to date. In addition, some systems offer connectivity to CICS, IMS on IBM systems, and also to other mainframes. Windows and X/Windows-based systems are also supported.

In the past, the work stations have typically been UNIX based, such as SUN SPARC work stations. More recently, Windows and OS/2 work stations are becoming more popular. Primarily because of the inherent flexibility of the systems, more variety will become apparent, as each organization uses those platforms most useful to it.

7.1.4   The Enhanced Client/Server Model

The model described here has been considerably simplified and is derived from that described in the X/Open DTP standard (1991), *Distributed Processing: Reference Model and Distributed Transaction Processing: The XA Specification.* Figure 7.2 is a depiction of the X/Open OLTP or, as designated here, enhanced client/server model.

The application program defines the operations to perform to accomplish the desired results. It defines the boundaries of the transaction and issues requests for service to the transaction manager, the communication manager, and one or more resource managers.

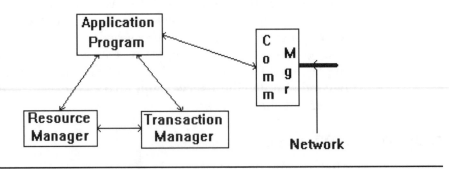

Figure 7.2   Enhanced client/server model.

The *resource manager* provides services that are provided within the transaction as requested by the application program. Typically, the resource manager is a database, but it may not always be so. Any updatable resource that must be maintained with transaction integrity must be managed by a resource manager, such as the queue to a money machine. Resource managers must provide two-phase commit services for the resource they are associated with.

The transaction manager provides services that manage transactions, including the two-phase commit among resource managers and the communication manager. If the transaction spans more than one platform, then one transaction manager involved with the transaction will be automatically designated the control transaction manager for the transaction.

The communication manager provides the interface to the communication services and manages the application level protocol. Generally, in client/server situations, the services provided are simply an interface to the data transport mechanism. Most enhanced client/server systems provide some type of conversational services, and it is the communications manager that provides these services.

This simplified view of the model will be referred to and expanded somewhat in the discussion of TUXEDO later in this chapter.

This model is partially supported by API specifications now existing from X/Open, which is continuing development of additional standards.

The resource manager is interfaced with the XA Specification from X/Open to provide necessary transaction management services supporting the enhanced client/server model. New specifications provide peer-to-peer interfaces and additional features for client/server. A number of database vendors now supply an XA interface for their products.

7.1.5 Available Products

There are three major vendors of enhanced client/server technology: TUXEDO from Novell's UNIX System Laboratories (USL), Encina from Transarc, and TopEnd from NCR.

TUXEDO, the oldest and most mature of the products, began as an in-house transaction processing system within AT&T and has been developed into a fully mature enhanced client/server and conversational manager. TUXEDO will be discussed fully later in this chapter and will be used as the example of enhanced client/server.

Encina, the newest of the offerings, was developed based on work done in the Computer Science Department at Carnegie Mellon University. Encina uses the distributed computing environment (DCE) developed by the Open Systems Foundation (OSF).

TopEnd was developed by NCR in the early 1990s as an entry into the open OLTP market, but when the design was completed, NCR found it had a fine enhanced client/server manager. It is available principally on NCR UNIX platforms but is in the process of being ported to other platforms.

7.2 OVERVIEW OF TUXEDO

TUXEDO is the result of more than ten years of development, first by Bell Laboratories and later by UNIX System Laboratories (USL), now owned by Novell. Initially the system was developed for internal use by AT&T but later became part of the UNIX offerings from USL. Release 4.0, made fully available in 1990, was the first release to offer full distributed transaction management capabilities, allowing reliable update use of databases on several platforms in the same transaction. Release 4.2.2, the latest version, offers a number of important features. TUXEDO adheres to all existing standards, most notably the XA Specification from X/Open.

7.2.1 Features of TUXEDO

TUXEDO is rich with features important to developing and using enhanced client/server applications:

- Implements the enhanced client/server model.
- Provides a fully distributed processing capability with transparent access to services from clients and other services.

- Provides both RPC and conversational client/server interaction between application processes.
- Provides a simplified API.
- Provides dynamic administration control and management of applications.
- Supports distributed computing using standard database interfaces to control two-phase commit.
- Allows specification of application password security and of user-provided authentication routines, such as Kerberos.
- Provides administrative control of data-dependent routing.
- Includes important development tools for use by C and COBOL programmers.
- Includes interfaces for development of work station and mainframe interfaces.
- Provides automatic translation of messages between clients and services and between services and services to support heterogeneous hardware.

TUXEDO also provides special support for work stations with its /WS feature:

- Client side API
- Support for UNIX, MS/DOS, MS/Windows and OS/2 work stations
- Additional security when accessing TUXEDO from nonsecure work stations

TUXEDO provides support for interfacing with mainframes, especially IBM MVS via CICS and IMS. /Host includes:

- Communication between UNIX based TUXEDO and MVS/CICS.
- Transparent data conversion between ASCII and EBCDIC.
- Ability to boot and shut down /Host services from the TUXEDO UNIX system.
- Ability to route requests to MVS/CICS services and/or UNIX-based TUXEDO services without regard to their location or type of platform.
- The same API for TUXEDO application programs to access MVS/CICS servers as it does for other TUXEDO servers.

7.2.2   How TUXEDO Works

Applications developed using C, COBOL, or a modern 4GL or object-oriented language all use the same basic approach to TUXEDO.

Client programs are ordinary programs that run in their environment exactly as if they were not TUXEDO clients, except that client programs:

- Issue a request to TUXEDO to join or leave a TUXEDO application.
- Issue requests for service to TUXEDO application servers.
- Have access to a number of useful TUXEDO tools and services once the program has joined the TUXEDO application.
- Can optionally communicate conversationally with servers.
- Client programs may be part of a *client group* that includes a resource manager participating with other resource managers in the commit controlled by the transaction manager.

Client programs may use any of the services offered by the platform they are running on except that they may not spawn another program while joined to TUXEDO. Also, it is not a good idea for a client program to access a database directly, even though it can be part of the transaction. Database access from a client cannot be routed by TUXEDO, and many other features are also lost.

Service programs are written as subroutines called from TUXEDO. TUXEDO provides the main line program for servers and calls them upon request. Service programs may use platform services as desired except that they should never spawn other programs, since service programs are always automatically joined with TUXEDO. Service programs may:

- Use interfaces and APIs provided by databases to access database services (including SQL), except they may never use any connect or transaction management provided by the database (this is done by TUXEDO via the standard database interface).
- Invoke other application services as if they were clients.
- Use all TUXEDO services.

- Communicate conversationally with clients and other services.
- Participate in TUXEDO transaction management with other services.

TUXEDO provides a network gateway in such a way that application program communication is transparent. In fact, some servers may be on the same platform as the client or may be remote. Also, it is possible during the life of the application for servers to be moved or for message routing to be administratively changed. All of this is completely transparent to the application program.

Figure 7.3 shows application clients requesting services via

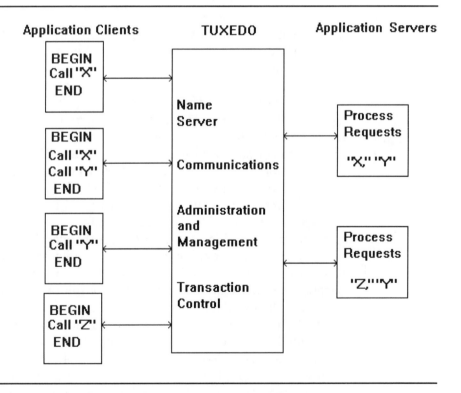

Figure 7.3   TUXEDO.

TUXEDO from application servers. Each client first issues a BEGIN request to TUXEDO, which signals that the client wants to begin processing a TUXEDO transaction. The client then issues one or more service requests. Using the name of the service, TUXEDO routes the request to the appropriate server.

The diagram indicates that a service may be provided by more than one server. If so, the application designer may use one of the following options to indicate to TUXEDO which server will provide the requested service:

- Allow TUXEDO to choose the server based on the current system load (load balancing).
- Indicate some value, contained in the service request data, that will be used to determine which server to use (data-dependent routing).

The routing options may be changed by the system administrator at any time without affecting either the application clients or service programs.

Within TUXEDO, the name server receives requests for service and determines the proper routing. The communications server will move the request using information provided by the name server. The destination server may be on the same platform as the client (unless the client is on a /WS work station or a /Host platform), or the destination may be anywhere in the network, as long as the destination platform is running TUXEDO.

Transaction control is invoked when the TUXEDO function tpbegin() is issued. The TUXEDO transaction manager maintains the transaction status until the transaction has been successfully completed or aborted. When the client issues a TUXEDO commit request, tpcommit(), transaction control ensures that all database updates have been reliably completed, via the XA interface with the databases used in the transaction.

TUXEDO administration management supports dynamic and static modification of the system configuration. Administration management can also be invoked in case of failure of part of the system—to attempt to continue functionality of the application, (though perhaps at a degraded performance level due to decreased resource availability) or to find and correct the problem.

7.2.3   Clients, Services, Servers, and Server Groups

In general, any program that requests a service from another program is a client, and the program that provides the service is a server. TUXEDO modifies this conceptual view of the relationship, in that TUXEDO applications include programs that may only request services, which are called clients in the TUXEDO nomenclature. The programs that provide the services are called servers, as expected. TUXEDO allows services to request service from other services, thus making it possible for a server to be a client in the general sense. TUXEDO never refers to a server as a client, though the services it provides may request services from another server.

TUXEDO treats clients differently from servers, and it is important to understand that a TUXEDO client is always only a client to TUXEDO and a server is always a server, no matter what type of processing is occurring.

Figure 7.4 shows the relationship of clients, services, servers,

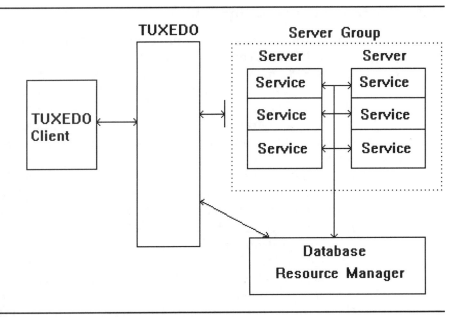

Figure 7.4   Clients, services, servers, and server groups.

and server groups. A *service* is that part of the *server* that provides a particular named service. A server may provide one or more services. A *server group* is a group of servers, identified to TUXEDO, that use a particular resource manager. Each server group may access zero or one resource manager. If it is desirable to access the same database from more than one server group, this is possible by identifying the resource manager as associated with each server group. Multiple types of databases (heterogeneous databases) can be used in the same TUXEDO application by establishing multiple server groups.

All of the servers within a server group must reside on the same platform and the server group must appear to TUXEDO to be on the same platform as the resource manager associated with it. Some databases provide distributed capabilities, so that the actual database may not be on the same platform as the server group. But as long as the database has the provision to provide an interface on the same platform as the server group, TUXEDO will consider the database to be on the same platform with it.

7.2.4 Notify and Conversational Mode

There are two modes of communication between clients and services: RPC and conversational.

In RPC mode, the client requests a service and receives a response. This is the only communication allowed between the client and service in this mode (except for notify, described later).

TUXEDO provides two other ways for clients and services to communicate: notify and conversational. Notify is used in RPC mode and allows a service to send an unsolicited message to a client that is programmed to receive such a message. The service uses the tpnotify() function to send a message to the client. The client can be notified immediately or when it next invokes a TUXEDO function. The choice is made administratively.

Conversational mode allows a TUXEDO process (a TUXEDO client or a TUXEDO service) to initiate a conversation with a service. Once the conversation is established, multiple messages may be exchanged without losing the context of either program. Conversations are terminated when either process in the conversation executes a TUXEDO return (tpreturn()) or commits the transaction (tpcommit()).

TUXEDO clients cannot initiate conversations with other TUXEDO clients.

7.3   PRINCIPLES OF DESIGN FOR TUXEDO

This section provides guidelines for designing and implementing an efficient enhanced client/server application in the TUXEDO environment. Sufficient information is provided to allow the reader to understand the mechanisms of TUXEDO and how they relate to the application. Some of the information is provided at the programming level, nonprogrammers nevertheless should be able to understand the principles.

It is not necessary to use COBOL or C to generate TUXEDO clients and servers. A number of 4GL and object-oriented products are available to accomplish this. These languages hide the details of TUXEDO from the developer, so it is not necessary to master the details, except as a means to understand the mechanisms of the platform to the extent necessary to create an efficient design. A later section will discuss the 4GL languages that work with TUXEDO.

7.3.1   The Client Program

The primary responsibility of the client program is to interface with the user. In most cases, the user will be a human being, so the client program is responsible for interacting with a person. However, the client program may interact with another computer or some sort of external device. This section will discuss the client program that interacts with the person, but the general principles will remain the same, no matter what part the client program plays in the application.

A well-designed client program will interact well with the user, use the services of TUXEDO and application services for any complex calculations or database interaction, and use the resources of the work station to meet these objectives.

The client program is initiated in the same way as any other program that runs on the platform. For instance, from UNIX or MS-DOS it may be from the command line and require typing the name of the program, such as "orders." In the case of Windows, it may be a DLL invoked when selected from a menu with a mouse. In any case, the client program runs in its environment without association with TUXEDO until it connects to TUXEDO with tpinit(). Once this function is called, the client may use those TUXEDO services allowed for a client and any application services it wishes.

The start and end of a transaction are controlled by the application. While it is not required, it is best to start and stop transactions within client programs. Therefore, the next TUXEDO service requested will normally be a transaction start (tpbegin()). The tpbegin() notifies TUXEDO that a transaction is beginning. At this point TUXEDO establishes a transaction identifier. Application programs need not be aware of the transaction identifier, since all use of it is reserved for TUXEDO.

After some processing and perhaps interaction with the user, the client will need services from application servers. The client then issues a tpcall(), which invokes the named service. The client provides the following with the tpcall() to invoke a service:

- Name of the service
- Location of the buffer containing information to be passed to the service program
- Length of the buffer passed to the service
- Location of the buffer where information returned from the service is to be stored by TUXEDO
- Length of the buffer provide to receive data

TUXEDO provides a service to allocate the proper buffers for use by the program in communicating with services.

The client has the choice of waiting for a response from the service request (synchronous operation, or blocking) or may use a form of tpcall (tpacall()), which allows the client to continue processing until it requires the response to continue (asynchronous, or nonblocking).

Generally the system should be designed to allow the client to make only a few service calls to process the application. The client program should be used primarily to interface with the user and should minimize the load on the network.

Once the client has completed its processing of a transaction by a combination of interaction with the user and required service calls, it then issues a "tpcommit" to complete the transaction reliably. TUXEDO handles all interaction with the databases to ensure reliable updating by the transaction, without application program involvement. The client will wait for the response, which will generally be "good," but the client should test the response in case there was a problem.

The client may wish to disassociate from TUXEDO at this point, though that is not required unless the client program is going to terminate. The client program issues a tpterm() to disassociate from TUXEDO.

7.3.2 The Server and Its Services

The server program provides the services required by the application. Each server may provide multiple services, with each service a subroutine called from the mainline provided by TUXEDO. Normally the name of the service is the same as the name of the subroutine that provides it. TUXEDO provides several methods to alias the service name, so that the name used in a request is not necessarily the same as that of the subroutine in the server providing the service. It is a good idea, generally, not to use the alias capability because of difficulty in maintaining the documentation necessary for maintenance and troubleshooting.

Servers process one request at a time. While servicing a request, the server cannot service another request, even for a different service. Each server may be providing services for multiple in-process transactions at the same time. After completing a service for transaction A, the server may provide service for transaction B before transaction A is complete. TUXEDO will maintain transaction integrity at all times, transparent to the application.

Designers should be careful when providing multiple services from the same server, since each server can provide service to one request at a time. The rule is that if a service will be highly used, it is a good idea to provide that service in a server by itself. Determining the proper mix of services in each server requires knowledge of how each service will be used, including the frequency of use and how long the service will take to process each request.

Multiple copies of a server can provide services to multiple requests at the same time. TUXEDO will automatically balance the load among the available servers. On a single processor platform, the following must be considered when planning to use multiple copies of servers:

- Memory requirements are minimal, since UNIX will use only one copy of the executable part of the program for multiple processes.
- Each process uses CPU cycles, even when not in use, because UNIX will search all processes in its list when starting actual execution (called *dispatching* or *context switching*).
- Generally services should be designed to perform the required service as quickly as possible. Necessary long-running services should be designed using other features of TUXEDO.

Servers are started when TUXEDO is booted. Each server may provide an optional initialization routine, which will be executed during start-up. During booting, TUXEDO will automatically connect to the database assigned to the server group using the open string designated by the database vendor and provided to TUXEDO by an administrative process. In this manner, servers with their services are made available to the system. Processes that are active but not actually executed until requested are often called *daemons* in UNIX jargon.

Servers are always connected to TUXEDO so there is no need to use the TUXEDO tpinit() function. Services have all the other TUXEDO services available as required to perform the service, including these:

- Requests to other services that return to the calling service as if it were a client (tpcall()).
- Requests to other services that pass along the control of the service and make the calling service available to accept another request (tpforward()).
- The ability to start and complete a transaction, if not already in a transaction (AUTOTRAN).
- Return results to the requester (tpreturn()).

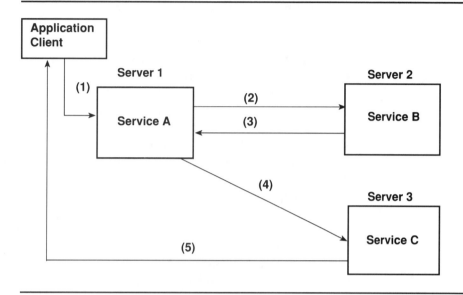

Figure 7.5   Service using other services.

Figure 7.5 illustrates how a service might use other services during execution on behalf of a request:

1. Server 1 receives a request for service A from a client.
2. After some processing, service A requests service B with the instruction to return the results.
3. Service B completes the service and returns the result to service A
4. Service B completes all the processing it is designed to do and passes the request to service C for completion.
5. Service C completes the processing of the original request and returns the result to the requester.

7.3.3   Server Groups

If there is only one database product used in the system and all the servers are on one platform, a single server group will be sufficient. Multiple server groups are required if there is more than one database product used or application servers reside on more than one platform. Beyond these hard rules, consideration should be given to how servers are grouped into server groups. Server groups may be migrated manually from one platform to another at any time, and they may be shut down or started. TUXEDO provides an administrative function to migrate server groups to another platform in the case of failure.

For these reasons, it is a good idea to provide necessary services in multiple server groups, especially with a large number of servers. Then some performance increase can be had and, more important, interruption to the application can be minimized by providing multiple server groups. There are at least two ways that multiple server groups can be used to improve performance and protect against certain kinds of failure.

If the system uses only one platform, then all servers are running on that platform and platform failure cannot be protected against. Spreading the servers among two or more server groups can improve performance in some cases and provide partial protection against momentary failure within one server group. Assuming that there is only one database, both server groups will connect to the database, and updates made via one server group will be seen properly by the other.

Since some databases provide single-threaded access, spreading the various servers among multiple server groups can have a dramatic effect on performance improvement.

If multiple platforms are being used, then each platform must have at least one server group. Usually in this case, the databases on the various platforms represent different sets of data. The simplest way to protect against full system failure is to spread the databases and tables among the servers such that the failure of one platform will not affect the operation of the remaining platforms. If there are multiple applications running, this technique can be very effective since it can be arranged so that only the application using a given platform will be affected by its failure.

Another method, one that is still simple and does not involve data replication, is to spread the data for an application among the platforms by horizontally partitioning the data. Using TUXEDO's data-dependent routing makes the location of the data transparent to all application programs, and the partitioning becomes a means of spreading the database load, thus increasing performance by using multiple platforms for the same application. In the case of a platform failure, only transactions using that section of data will be affected.

If the data has been horizontally partitioned among multiple platforms and one platform fails, and providing provision has been made for replication, then TUXEDO can be instructed by an administrator to send service requests to an alternate platform, keeping the system fully operational though perhaps at a lower performance due to the lost resource.

7.3.4 TUXEDO Buffers

Information accompanying requests for service and responses from services are passed in special TUXEDO typed buffers, data structures defined by application designers and made known to TUXEDO. There are a number of predefined buffer types provided by the system, and they are sufficient for most applications, but TUXEDO also provides support for user-defined buffer types. TUXEDO typed buffers are defined by the programmer using special TUXEDO utilities. Buffer allocation in a program is done with a buffer allocation request to TUXEDO (tpalloc()). Buffer types include:

- STRING: A null-terminated character array.
- CARRAY: An array of uninterpreted binary data.
- VIEW: A C-structure.
- FML: A special TUXEDO type in which each field carries its own definition.

All buffer types except CARRAY support automatic translation of data between differing platforms. CARRAY is designed for sending binary data where translation is not desirable. The VIEW buffer type is designed for use in C programs to facilitate ease of programming. The FML buffer type is the most flexible and should be used for most applications.

FML (fielded manipulation language) buffers have some important features that make them especially useful for building efficient, flexible programs:

- The language facilitates buffer definition. This language allows using multiple data types in the same buffer.

- FML buffers are automatically sized when used, so although many fields are defined, only the fields actually populated are sent in a given message.
- New fields can be added to an FML buffer without affecting existing programs (clients and services). Only the programs that use the new fields must be changed.
- FML buffers can be used by any program in addition to TUX-EDO clients and services (when made available via the TUX-EDO libraries).
- FML buffers support arrays of fields, with automatic sizing of messages depending on the number of occurrences of each field.

Buffers other than FML buffers should be sized minimally. That is, they should be made as small as possible and still contain sufficient information. Some compromise between providing too many different buffers (complexity) and keeping buffers small (resource use) will be necessary. Buffer design is an important but often overlooked part of designing for systems such as TUX-EDO. Each application should be analyzed carefully, including developing data flow diagrams for requests, in order to make efficient use of this powerful tool.

TUXEDO provides automatic translation of data when its messages pass between platforms (except for the CARRAY buffer type). This feature is extremely important when the network contains heterogeneous hardware. The translation includes not only between UNIX and UNIX and work station and server, but also between ASCII and EBCDIC. This translation is controlled by the way buffers are defined to the system.

7.3.5 Heterogeneous Databases

If the enterprise wishes to use database products from more than one vendor, the system must provide for use of heterogeneous databases. TUXEDO eases use of heterogeneous databases in the same application.

The simplest situation occurs when certain tables are on one type of database and other tables are on another. It is easy to provide for separate server groups for each type of database and provide the appropriate services on the proper database.

If a logical database, such as the customer master, is stored partially in different types of databases, it is difficult with most system tools to maintain performance and still provide full functionality among the heterogeneous databases. Using data-dependent routing, TUXEDO can provide the same services for each database, transparently to all clients in the system.

Figure 7.6 illustrates how heterogeneous databases can be accommodated using TUXEDO. Service 1 updates the customer database. Suppose that customers with certain customer numbers are on database A, and the rest are on database B. Service 1 must do certain application processing before actually updating the database. It may be that during this processing it must access the current customer information and, after processing, update the proper database. When service 1 requires data from the customer database it issues a service request to the service named CUSTSQL. The service CUSTSQL is provided in two servers as service 2 and service 3. Service 1 issues a TUXEDO request for

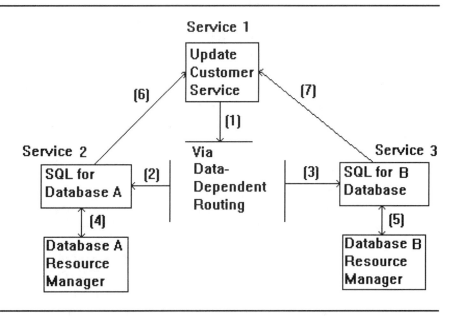

Figure 7.6   Heterogeneous databases.

retrieval (not using SQL) to CUSTSQL, (arrow 1). Data-dependent routing looks at the customer number in the passed buffer and routes the request to either service 2 or service 3 (arrows 2 and 3). Services 2 and 3 are each written specifically to access database A or database B and are in separate server groups. These services issue the proper SQL to their own database and receive the response, (arrows 4 and 5). When they issue the request to return the response, it will return directly to service 1. Service 1 will receive the correct response without being concerned with the type of database used. Updates are accomplished in the same manner.

7.3.6   Using Parallel Computers

Parallel computers are becoming more prevalent. Because TUXEDO provides for building servers that act independently and manages the transaction integrity among the servers, programming to take best advantage of the SMP capability of modern parallel computers is as simple as programming for a single processor platform.

SMP attempts to keep a process running in the same processor as much as possible. By designing efficient servers, the designer can be ensured that parallelism will be maximized and cache thrashing and other overhead will be minimized. It turns out that efficient application design for TUXEDO is the same no matter what platform is used, so if a system is running well on a single processor platform, it will run linearly better on an SMP platform.

Some computer manufacturers are producing massively parallel systems with 1024 or more processors. Many of these systems have the logical look of separate computers, where the computers are linked with a high-speed internal bus. Although these systems use an operating system with a method similar in many ways to SMP, the system does not completely succeed in presenting the same look as a single processor while maintaining full usage of its power. On these machines, TUXEDO can support a design that will take full advantage of the hardware design by placing TUXEDO servers on individual processors and allowing the TUXEDO system to balance the load. If some system like

TUXEDO is not used, designing efficient use of the hardware becomes much more difficult.

7.4   TUXEDO AND DATABASES

7.4.1 Transactions

X/Open provides a standardized interface between transaction managers and resource managers (resource managers are usually databases) called the XA Specification. This specification provides for the communication required between the transaction manager and the database to control transaction integrity.

When a transaction is started, a global transaction identifier, the XID, is created for the internal use of the transaction manager. Whenever any application server invokes database services, the transaction manager stores that fact along with the XID. When the transaction is terminated, the transaction manager uses the XA Specification interface to communicate with the database to terminate the database transaction. When the application requests a commit and more than one server group was involved in the transaction, the transaction manager will use a *presumed abort two-phase* commit protocol (see Appendix D) to complete the transaction with ensured transaction integrity. The transaction manager cooperates with the databases to accomplish the two-phase commit.

When only one server group is involved in a transaction, TUXEDO considers it a *local transaction*. The transaction manager will not use two phase commit with a local transaction.

If more than one server group is involved in a transaction, on the same platform or not, TUXEDO will consider it a *distributed transaction* and use the two-phase commit protocol. Generally a transaction is considered distributed only when more than one platform is involved. In fact, any system must consider a transaction distributed if more than one resource is involved, on the same platform or not. TUXEDO detects this distribution automatically.

7.4.2   Designing to Prevent Unnecessary Program Changes

TUXEDO allows a design that will require few, if any, program changes if the database type, the database location, or the organization is changed. The rule is to keep all database access separate from the main processing, using servers dedicated to database access. If there are changes involving the database, any necessary program changes will be isolated to the database access servers.

In many instances, such as change of database location, no programming changes will be required because TUXEDO makes such changes transparent to the program. Relatively simple administrative changes are all that are required. This applies particularly to horizontally partitioned tables. Using data-dependent routing, the administrator can cause the proper routing to occur, transparent to the program.

7.4.3   Using Database Integrity Features

Many modern database products provide a number of integrity features, such as data type checking, data range checking, referential integrity checking, and uniqueness checks.

Data type and data range checking usually are done using the data dictionary local to the table being updated. These types of checks work satisfactorily in any environment, including client/server distributed systems.

Great care must be exercised before using database referential checking if more than one platform is used in the system. When the database checks referential integrity, it will need to access the controlling table to be sure that the required value or values are present. If the controlling table is not present on the platform where the check is required, the database must use its distribution capability to accomplish the check. It is best to avoid using the database-provided distribution capability. Instead of using the database referential integrity check when multiple platforms are involved, perform the check in the application server. TUXEDO will automatically route the retrieval required to the proper platform.

For performance reasons, it is important to use the database uniqueness capability as much as possible. When a table is partitioned, with certain values on one platform and other values on another, the tables should be designed so that any values requiring uniqueness are on the same platform. For instance, to ensure unique customer numbers, include a platform location code in the customer number or assign a range of numbers to each platform. The database will then ensure uniqueness on each platform, and the design of the customer number will guarantee overall uniqueness.

7.4.4 Joins

When the application requires matched data from more than one table, it is a join. If the tables being joined are on the same platform, the database will create the join efficiently. If the join involves more than one platform, no database will perform the join as efficiently as the application program. Performance will be much improved when the features of TUXEDO are used to access individual databases as required.

There is some controversy about joins in the distributed environment. Many knowledgeable people believe that, joins over the network are to be avoided. If the system is small, there are few users, and networked joins are seldom invoked, then the simplification provided by the database join may be worth the savings in development cost (which are minimal). In all other cases, especially where performance is important, the joins should be done in the application program.

7.4.5 Database Distribution Features

Modern databases provide for distributing the database, placing various tables on multiple platforms, and making access to these tables transparent. At first glance, this simplification of access seems highly desirable. Unfortunately, these systems cannot provide the required performance at anything near the cost that can be attained using a system like TUXEDO and accessing each individual location with a local TUXEDO server.

The distributed database must use a distributed data dictionary and multiple high-traffic accesses to the network. The network load increases, and, particularly in the case of WANs, the cost to provide the bandwidth necessary soon escalates. The system described in the next chapter provides a good illustration of this situation, especially when compared with the system designed using only database vendor tools.

7.4.6 Data Replication

Some enterprises require protection of data beyond simple backups. Often this requirement is to allow restarting the system from a known point without the need to do a time-consuming restoration of the database. To provide for this capability, the database is duplicated, and the duplicate is kept up to date as closely to the active copy as possible. This method is called *data replication*. Data replication has these important characteristics:

- The copy must perfectly reflect the active version up to a well-known point in time.
- The number of updates done to the active version that are not done to the replicated version must be minimized (the difference is often called the *delta*).
- An accurate log of the updates not yet completed on the inactive version is kept.
- An automated method is in place to bring the inactive copy up to date in case of a failure that makes the active version unavailable.
- An automated method is in place to switch to the backup version.

TUXEDO provides a number of features that facilitate a data replication plan meeting the needs of most situations. The primary capabilities are discussed here but not all of the details of how it is done. The sample system described in the next chapter provides additional information.

The primary features of TUXEDO that can be used are guaranteed transaction integrity and recovery, reliable queues, and relatively easy switching to backup servers.

Guaranteed transaction integrity provides the ability to log the completion of a transaction with accuracy and the ability to notify users of transaction completion. Each user can therefore be sure of which entries have completed correctly, providing a manual backup (by reentering failed transactions) in case of catastrophe. Services can use transaction integrity to maintain updated logs ensured to be accurate. These logs can be used to update the backup version to the point of failure.

The reliable queue feature allows a server to enter the updates on a processing queue that will be used by other servers to update the backup copy on the fly. Once the information is entered into the queue and the transaction has been successfully completed, the system will guarantee that the entries on the queue will be there for use at any time, until they have been successfully processed. As the entries on the queue are retrieved for processing, the queue process can start another independent transaction to ensure that the entry is properly processed before being removed from the queue. This method ensures the accuracy of the backup copy.

The queue for backup processing can be maintained on a different platform from the primary processing, allowing backup copy updating to occur even if the primary processing platform fails. Also, backup updating can continue to completion after the primary failure, leaving the backup copy complete up to the last successful transaction. Using this method, users can begin with the first failed transaction and bring the backup copy up to date.

When the primary platform fails, it is important to switch to the backup platform as quickly as possible while maintaining the integrity and accuracy of the database. This requirement can be met in two ways. If the server group is run on two platforms and one platform fails, TUXEDO will detect the failure and send requests for services from the server group to the platform where the service is still functional. If the server group is run on one platform with another platform designated as the backup, the server group can be administratively migrated to the other platform in case of failure.

It is possible for the migration and restart procedures to fail if the system failure is more widespread than a simple platform failure (such as failure of the complete network or a power outage that makes all server platforms inoperable). In this case, the recovery capabilities will allow the user to recover all in-flight transactions to a known state: complete or failed. The system will inform the user of which transactions failed and which completed successfully during recovery. The recovery includes recovering the reliable queues (that is why they are called reliable) so that updating the backup copy can continue accurately once the appropriate platforms and communications have been restored.

7.5 TUXEDO AND WORK STATIONS

7.5.1 The TUXEDO Work Station Product

The TUXEDO work station product (/WS) provides access to all TUXEDO features without loading the work station with the overhead of the full system. It provides a smaller part of TUXEDO in order to allow it to run in an environment with fewer resources. A number of useful tools for developing end user interfaces are available for /WS, including window system tools.

Figure 7.7 illustrates /WS. Each work station has a gateway

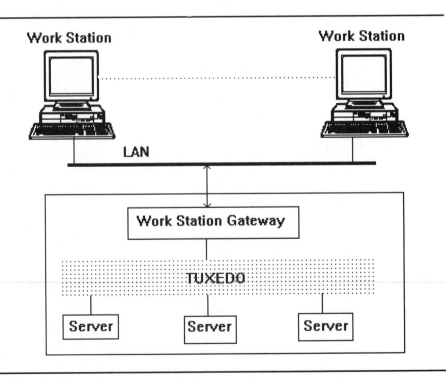

Figure 7.7   /WS architecture.

that connects via the LAN to the gateway in a UNIX server. Each work station TUXEDO client has access to the full services of TUXEDO as described and can access any service in the network.

Since /WS costs less per work station than a full system and smaller work stations cost less than larger ones, using /WS on the work stations can be very cost-effective. Fortunately, using work stations on a LAN with /WS provides very good performance, to the point where there is no significant difference from using the entire system on a LAN.

The /WS feature can be used on a WAN and in the right circumstances can be very effective. /WS should be used directly on the WAN when:

- There are few work stations at a remote location.
- Using the local server for a particular application is not cost-effective.
- The system is under test, and it is not desirable to use a local server.
- The work station has sufficient disk space to store the system and the application programs.

7.5.2 UNIX Work Stations

UNIX work stations can be very powerful; they:

- Can provide multiple user access to a single work station.
- Provide X/Windows-based GUI interfaces.
- Usually are on powerful computers.
- Are capable of running complex user interface calculations while providing good performance.

/WS provides a solution to providing access for UNIX work stations to a TUXEDO-based application.

If the work station is diskless and is connected to an LAN-based file server, /WS will work with good performance characteristics since it does not require a large amount of program reloading.

/WS supports multiple users with a multithreaded gateway; therefore it does not load UNIX with multiple processes as more users are added. In some cases, using TUXEDO and /WS will improve performance over other methods because of the decreased number of UNIX processes.

7.5.3   PC Work Stations

/WS supports MS-DOS, Windows, Windows/NT, and OS/2. MS-DOS and Windows usually are single-user work stations. OS/2 is sometimes used to support multiple users on the PC. With Windows and OS/2, single users may start multiple transactions that overlap. /WS provides a multithreaded gateway for these platforms and thus does not overload the system with overhead.

/WS provides support for building GUI applications on these platforms, so that the presentation of information can be very user friendly. Using /WS allows the system designer to assign user display processing to the work station and number crunching to the server, improving control and performance.

7.6   OVERVIEW OF TUXEDO ADMINISTRATION

TUXEDO is administered by manipulating the values in two files: UBBCONFIG, an ASCII file that can be modified with any text editor, and TUXCONFIG, binary file generated by TUXEDO. TUXCONFIG can be created (or recreated) in its entirety using UBBCONFIG as input, or it can be modified directly using TUXEDO interactive administration tools.

TUXEDO is administered and monitored using three methods:

1. Off-line modification of UBBCONFIG with the text editor of choice.
2. On-line interactive modification of the running system, including shutting down and bringing up new servers and services.
3. On-line modification of the system configuration.

The procedure for creating the initial configuration and making modifications is:

1. Create an initial UBBCONFIG and TUXCONFIG.
2. Use the interactive tools to make necessary changes to TUXCONFIG, in most cases while the system is still running.

3. Use a TUXEDO utility to store a backup of the new parameters in UBBCONFIG.

The items that cannot be changed with the system running are those that could affect an in-flight transaction. In many cases, these changes can still be made on-line by first shutting down the part of the system that will be affected. For instance, new servers and new services can be added at any time, but servers and their services cannot be removed without first shutting down the affected servers.

7.6.1 Administration Tools

Off-line Tools Off-line modification is completed using the following steps:

1. Modify UBBCONFIG with a text editor.
2. Create a TUXCONFIG binary version using the utility tmloadcf.
3. Reboot TUXEDO to apply the changes.

This method is usually used to configure the system initially and to make major changes to the configuration. The interactive utilities described later will be used to make changes with the system running.

The following utilities are used to manage other aspects:

- tmunloadcf reads the binary configuration file, TUXCONFIG, and creates UBBCONFIG.
- tmboot boots TUXEDO.
- tmshutdown shuts TUXEDO down.

Monitoring the System and Modifying Service Availability
The utility tmadmin provides interactive services on a running system, including:

- Information on available servers, including their configuration.
- Examining a number of statistics, such as number of requests outstanding on a server, rate of service requests, number of transactions completed, and the status of service queues.
- Moving servers from one platform to another.

- Starting new servers and making their services available.
- Moving all services from one platform to another in a block.
- Shutting down individual servers or all servers on a platform.

Changes made by tmadmin become effective as soon as they are completed but are not permanent; they will not be in effect on the next system start after the system is shut down.

tmadmin is also useful for finding and correcting problems. It is especially helpful if a portion of the network fails, since it can be used to find the failed part of the system and replace it with a backup system without taking the entire system down.

Changing the System Configuration On-line TUXEDO provides the interactive utility tmconfig to examine and modify the system configuration file interactively while the system is running. Changes made by tmconfig are permanent because tmconfig directly modifies the binary version of the configuration in TUXCONFIG.

All elements of the system configuration can be examined with tmconfig. Changes that can be added or modified while the system is running include:

- Modifying network addresses.
- Changing certain elements of the server or services configuration, such as adding copies of servers and changing priorities.
- Adding new entries to the configuration to make the addition of servers and services permanent.
- Adding new platforms and all related configuration entries.

Changes made using tmconfig become effective the next time the system is started.

7.6.2 An Administration Example

Suppose that a new platform is to be added to an existing system to provide additional capacity. The user does not want to shut the system down to provide the new capacity and thus takes the following steps:

1. Examines the running system with tmadmin to be sure that the system is executing as expected.

2. Examines the current configuration using tmconfig to be sure that the configuration is set as expected.

3. Adds the proper configuration for the new platform, including limitations of the servers, so that they do not affect the running system.

4. Boots the new platform using the tmboot option that boots only the desired platform without affecting the running system.

5. Runs a test of the new platform to be sure that it is on-line properly.

6. Uses tmadmin to make the new servers available.

7. Uses tmconfig to modify the configuration to set TUXCONFIG so that the next system start will make them generally available.

8. Run tmunloadcf to create a new UBBCONFIG for backup.

After these procedures are completed, users will have access to services on the new platform, and the system configuration will be backed up for future use, if required. The additional capacity will increase the performance, while system activity was not affected during the process of adding the new platform.

7.7   USING TUXEDO WITH A MAINFRAME

TUXEDO provides a generalized gateway called /HOST designed specifically to allow use of interfaces with any other transaction management system, including any required data conversion such as between ASCII and EBCDIC. Using /HOST, a user need only create a gateway for the desired system, allowing TUXEDO to access and use servers running on the proprietary platforms in the same manner as if they were on a UNIX platform. Servers provided by /HOST are available transparently to all TUXEDO clients and administered from TUXEDO in the same manner as any other servers.

One vendor, Information Management Company, provides Open Transport for MVS, which gives full TUXEDO connectivity with MVS platforms using IMS and CICS. The IMS version of Open Transport for MVS routes the transaction to MVS via TCP/IP and places it in the IMS transaction queue. Only one Open

Transport for MVS is required in the network, and any number of UNIX platforms and their counterpart MVS servers may be configured by the customer to meet access and performance requirements. The CICS version operates in a similar manner.

Using gateways such as Open Transport for MVS allows the TUXEDO user to access and modify DB2, IMS, VSAM, or other databases stored on MVS platforms while maintaining full transaction integrity and server management capabilities provided by TUXEDO.

7.8   ADVANTAGES OF ENHANCED CLIENT/SERVER SYSTEMS

TUXEDO, and the other enhanced client/server systems mentioned (often called transaction processing systems), offer a large number of advantages for full enterprise client/server computing. They are:

- Distribute processing, not just data.
- Use servers to maximum advantage.
- Allow using heterogeneous databases without major program changes.
- Dramatically decrease network traffic.
- Reconfigure the network without requiring application program changes.
- Improve scalability to take advantage of more computing power without application program changes.
- Interface with RDBMSs in a standardized way.
- Allow adding new RDBMS systems with minimal disruption and program changes.
- Provide a fully integrated enterprise-wide solution to distributed processing.
- Provide departmental and central control and accountability, even when using distributed data.
- Work with mixed networks (LANS and WANS) without program changes.
- Provide great flexibility when choosing platforms on which to implement applications.
- Simplify administration with dynamic application configuration and system tuning.

7.9   DISADVANTAGES OF ENHANCED CLIENT/SERVER SYSTEMS

It is difficult to find disadvantages to the enhanced client/server system method, which appears to be the optimal solution available for large client/server systems. Some have perceived the following as disadvantages:

- Currently there are a limited number of enhanced 4GL and Case tools available for development in the Enhanced Client/ Server environment
- The technology is not well known (though it will become standard soon, with recognition of X/Open distributed transaction processing).

All current users are very satisfied, but there are not as many users of this enhanced client/server as there are database server users, though more businesses are finding this environment necessary as they gain experience.

8

A Sample Application
for TUXEDO

This chapter describes the same order entry system as used for the database example in Chapter 6, but using TUXEDO in addition to a modern relational database. The system requirements are described in Appendix A; the network architecture is described in Appendix B.

Using TUXEDO, no compromises of the requirements will be necessary. The system will be described here with some of the details missing, but all essential information will be presented.

8.1   THE DATABASE

8.1.1   Data Requirements

The database is the same as that described for the database server example, except that the tables will be partitioned and replicated. The database will consist of the following tables:

- Customer (containing customer addresses, special discount information, etc.)
- Inventory master (containing product description, price information, etc.)

- Warehouse stock levels (containing the inventory levels for each warehouse)
- Accounts receivable (containing customer's aged balances)
- Order header (containing the customer number, the order status, the shipping address for this order, the customer purchase order number, and other miscellaneous information common to the entire order)
- Order detail (containing the item number, the quantity ordered, the price per item, discount given, etc.)

8.1.2 Database Definitions

The customer table was created with the following SQL statement:

```
CREATE TABLE CUSTOMER
      UNIQUE CUSTNO CHAR(8) NOT NULL,
      CUSTNAME CHAR(35),
      CUSTADD1 CHAR(35),
      CUSTADD2 CHAR(35),
      CUSTADD3 CHAR(35),
      CUSTADD4 CHAR(35),
      CUSTCITY CHAR(25),
      CUSTZIP CHAR(10),
      CUSTDISC CHAR(1),
      CUSTDPER NUMERIC(4,2);
```

The inventory table was created with this statement:

```
CREATE TABLE INVENTORY
      UNIQUE INVNUM CHAR(12) NOT NULL,
      INVNAM CHAR(15),
      INVBPRCE NUMERIC(3,6),
      INVDCD1 CHAR(1),
      INVDQTY1 INTEGER,
      INVDPER1 NUMERIC(4,2),
      INVDCD2 CHAR(1),
      INVDQTY2 INTEGER,
      INVDPER2 NUMERIC(4,2),
      INVDCD3 CHAR(1),
      INVDQTY3 INTEGER,
      INVDPER3 NUMERIC(4,2);
```

The warehouse stock level table was created with this statement:

```
CREATE TABLE STKLEV
      UNIQUE WREHSE CHAR(4) NOT NULL,
      WRESTKNUM CHAR(15),
      WRELEV INTEGER;
```

The order header table was created with this statement:

```
CREATE TABLE ORDHEAD
      UNIQUE ORDNUM CHAR(7) NOT NULL,
      ORDCUST CHAR(8),
      ORDCPO CHAR(20),
      ORDEDATE DATE,
      CUSTNAME CHAR(35),
      ORDSADD1 CHAR(35),
      ORDSADD2 CHAR(35),
      ORDSADD3 CHAR(35),
      ORDSADD4 CHAR(35),
      ORDSCITY CHAR(25),
      ORDSZIP CHAR(10),
      ORDSTAT CHAR(1);
```

The first two characters of the order number will be the office code; the rest of the number will be assigned sequentially by the system.

The order line item table was created with this statement:

```
CREATE TABLE ORDLINE
      UNIQUE LINONUM CHAR(7) NOT NULL,
      LINNO INTEGER,
      LINITEM CHAR(12),
      LINQTY INTEGER,
      LINDCD CHAR(1),
      LINDPER NUMERIC(4,2),
      LINSTAT CHAR(1),
      LINWRE CHAR(4);
```

The accounts receivable table is defined by the accounts receivable system. The aged balance and credit code will be used by the order entry system to determine the creditworthiness of the customer.

8.1.3   Table Partitioning

The company has determined that the preponderance of orders likely to be received at a given branch office will come from a set of zip codes. The tendency will be reinforced because the company will make certain toll-free telephone numbers available to each branch office only for customers in selected zip areas. Therefore, the customer master and accounts receivable tables will be partitioned by the first three numbers of the zip code. The construction of the customer number will preserve uniqueness without querying the entire database.

The warehouse stock level table will be maintained at each warehouse and accessed there as orders are entered.

8.1.4   Data Replication

The company is comfortable with the partitioned database but requires that updates to the customer master be available locally at the central office for other purposes. A short lag in this updating is acceptable.

Any updates to the customer master originating at any branch office or at the home office will be forwarded to the home office and the proper branch office using reliable queues.

8.1.5   Order History

Orders with open items will be maintained at the individual branch offices. Weekly, a program at the home office will examine the order tables in all branches, using the order shipment database stored in the warehouses to find and transfer closed orders to the home office and delete the closed orders from the branch office tables. The home office closed order table will serve as an order history table. An adjunct subsystem (not described here) will direct queries about orders to either the local branch office for service or to the order history table at the home office.

8.2 SYSTEM DESIGN

8.2.1 System Design Considerations

The database will be designed using the following assumptions:

- A 10 Mb LAN.
- A 56 Kb WAN.
- There is sufficient computing power in the servers and work stations to make the network the deciding factor in performance.
- Average or "normal" usage is by 30 simultaneous users.
- The system must be designed to handle three orders per second and allow for short peak loads up to five orders per second.
- The average order has ten line items.

8.2.2 The Design

Figure 8.1 illustrates the TUXEDO order entry components at each branch office. The work stations will use a set of TUXEDO client programs that interact with each other and the user via the chosen GUI interface. These clients will use services provided by servers at the local server platform.

From the client program viewpoint, all services are provided by local servers. When an order is received at a branch office that does not have the customer in its local database, data-dependent routing will be used to transfer all service requests to the branch office, where the customer master data resides. That branch office will become the controlling branch as if the order originated there, transparent to the user, except that the branch office code will appear on the order. There are two layers of servers: the functional servers, which provide the necessary functions, and the database access servers, which contain the appropriate database interface calls.

Since stock levels are maintained at the individual warehouses, the inventory manager at the branch office will invoke a server at the chosen warehouse to obtain stock availability and to update the stock level as each order is completed.

The replicated tables at the home office are maintained by use of reliable queues invoked from the database access servers.

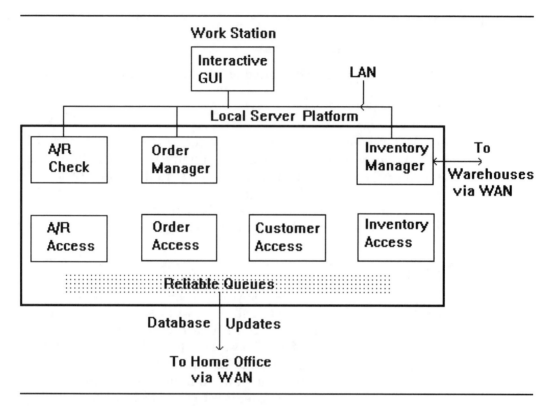

Figure 8.1   System/T components at branch offices.

8.2.3 The Load on the WAN

Using this design, the only WAN use on each order is for stock checking and level maintenance. The following messages will be placed on the WAN:

- A service request to the primary warehouse location for stock level for each item.
- Results returned from the warehouse.
- Up to two conditional stock requests to other warehouses if the stock level is insufficient to meet the order requirements at the first warehouse chosen.

- A single message when the order is completed to indicate that the order is to be shipped.

One message will be sent for the order containing a list of stock numbers with a quantity required for each. The size of this message will be 10 times 12 (the length of an item number) plus 10 times 4 (the size of an integer for the quantity) plus the overhead for TUXEDO of 300 bytes, for a total message size of 460 bytes. The return message will contain 10 times 12 plus 10 (1 byte indicator of stock level for each item) plus the overhead for TUXEDO, for a total of 430 bytes. The total amount of data transmitted is then 890 bytes per order, or 7120 bits per order. During normal load, the WAN is carrying 3 times 7120 or 21,360 bits per order. If the load reaches 5 orders per second, the load becomes 35,600 bits per second, well within the capacity of the WAN.

If the stock level is insufficient to fill the order of a given line item, the stock check service at the warehouse will forward the request to its alternate. The alternate will forward to the third warehouse if necessary. Since the company intends to maintain full stock at each warehouse, it estimates that stock shortages will occur less than 1 percent of the time and has chosen to accept this potential extra network load as inconsequential.

Updates of the replicated data in the home office will also travel over the WAN. These updates represent a minimal load. At peak times, these updates may fall behind, but the overall loading is such that they will quickly catch up.

Because there is the potential of requiring a full download of the order tables for statistical analysis, the company will set up the WAN for a 16-hour, 5-day service. The 4 extra hours at the end of the day will be more than sufficient to perform any processing required.

8.2.4 How the System Will Work

As orders are entered, processing will proceed as follows:

1. The customer master will be accessed to verify customer information.

2. The order header will be created.
3. As each line item is created, general information about the item will be retrieved locally.
4. When all line items have been entered, the availability of the items will be checked at the warehouse.
5. The ordered quantity will be put on hold at the selected warehouse.
6. When the availability has been checked with the warehouse and the customer has okayed the order, the system will check accounts receivable.
7. If the accounts receivable check is acceptable, the order will be completed, with a message to the selected warehouse to ship the order.
8. The transaction will be committed.

Note that the hold on the warehouse is part of the transaction and will be committed when the transaction is committed or removed automatically if the transaction is aborted.

Order status queries will be processed by an adjunct system that will:

1. Retrieve the order using data-dependent routing to access the correct branch office order tables.
2. Invoke a service at the warehouses in a manner similar to when the order was entered to retrieve shipping information.
3. Present the information to the user.

8.2.5   Development Languages

The company could have chosen to write the system using a 4GL from the limited number compatible with TUXEDO. For a number of reasons, the company probably will choose to write the user interface in some type of modern, object-oriented, high-level language and write the servers in COBOL or C.

TUXEDO clients can be written in any language that allows direct calling of functions, so the choice for the clients will depend largely on personal preference and the ability of the language to support development of the GUI front end.

8.3   COMMENTS ON THE SYSTEM

This design will perform well using the lowest-cost WAN. It will provide the enterprise with all required features, at reasonable administrative costs.

It is important to note that using only a database server, use of partitioned tables is not feasible because of the difficulty of administration. In this case, all tables have the same name and definition. Their location is fixed but transparent to the application programs. New locations can be added or the partitioning parameters changed simply by moving data and programs and making a few administrative changes to the data-dependent routing parameters of TUXEDO. Thus, this system can operate with most data located locally but fully and transparently available to all nodes in the system.

An additional feature provided by this system, but not necessarily obvious, is that each server may use a database from a different vendor. In fact, the tables on each server may be from different vendors. This ability could save time and money if each branch office had previously purchased a different database for local use.

Mention of the type of work station has been deliberately left out of the description. Most likely the work stations will be Windows platforms. If any other work station type proves desirable in the future, it will be a simple matter to move TUXEDO to the new platform and run. Of course, the work stations may be of various types from the beginning, and TUXEDO will not be affected. Only the capability of the development language to operate on various types of platforms is a factor in moving the system from platform to platform.

9

Help for Legacy Systems

There are two major problems to moving computing systems to new environments:

- The investment in the current system may be large, and it may not be desirable to finance a reengineering of the system.
- The cost of training personnel in new technology may be very large.

Most of the current investment is in systems designed to run on mainframes. Most often when the mainframe is mentioned, people mean the IBM MVS system. Since MVS systems make up the largest component of legacy systems, most efforts at providing migration tools have been for that platform. This chapter will concentrate on describing tools for migrating MVS, but many of these tools may also be useful for migration from platforms provided by other mainframe vendors. The two primary migration paths are to move old systems to the new using tools that make the cost of moving reasonable or continue to use the old systems where they are, but make the data in the old systems available to the new systems.

In either case, most users will be intending to convert their computing systems to newer technology eventually. The time to move completely to newer platforms and paradigms will vary greatly among users. Some will work to eliminate their older systems as fast as possible, perhaps within a year or two; others will want to spread out the time to allow proper amortization of development costs and to acquire the technology gradually. Others will replace their old systems totally. For some, this may be the wisest and most economical choice. But even in these cases, knowledge of the migration tools is essential before embarking on such a large undertaking, so that the proper choices may be made and to provide information so that backup procedures can be in place on the chance that only part of the new system will be working in a timely fashion.

While personnel will eventually require retraining, moving the systems from the mainframe to new platforms using special translation and simulation tools will provide some of the benefits of new technology immediately while allowing a manageable period of adjustment and training for user and development personnel. These are the people who will continue to use tools such as COBOL and CICS. Since modernized, open-systems versions of both COBOL and CICS are being made available, it may prove practical in some cases to remain with these tools.

This chapter will discuss the tools available, with comments on how each tool can help with one or more of the situations noted.

9.1   USING LEGACY DATA

Legacy data on MVS systems can be accessed by use of products such as Open TransPort from Information Management Company. This product allows making databases on MVS systems an integral part of new systems running in the client/server environment and, in fact, makes the mainframe a server to the system.

Most relational database vendors, such as Informix, Oracle, and Sybase, provide tools to help with conversion of DB2 tables. If it is necessary to move the data off the mainframe and the data is not already in a relational database, most likely a conversion program will be needed.

If the system is written in COBOL using SQL for data access, it may be possible to move the source to the new platform and recompile to get a working system. This still leaves the problem of moving the existing data to the new system.

There are VSAM equivalents available for UNIX that can be used for VSAM databases. Moving the data to them may be as simple as running a backup utility on MVS and using the resultant files as input to a conversion utility on UNIX, but in some cases conversions programs must be written.

IMS databases are difficult to convert to UNIX, and there are few, if any, reliable IMS equivalents available for UNIX.

9.2 COBOL

From the mid-1960s to the mid-1980s, COBOL was the language of choice for nearly all business system development. Even today there is considerable development using COBOL. The language has been greatly improved over the years, and a large pool of skilled people who can develop systems. For these reasons, CO-BOL will continue to be important for maintenance of old systems and for some continued development.

There are good COBOL compilers available for UNIX, most notably from Microfocus. The enterprise can use these compilers to move COBOL applications to UNIX, but they are not magic. Before systems will run well on UNIX, organizations must:

- Convert the job control language (JCL) to the UNIX equivalents, which are some combination of execution scripts called *Shell Scripts* (similar to TSO CLISTs); use of a utility called *awk,* which provides a comprehensive language for manipulating data and execution flow; additional programs to improve efficiency.
- Make changes in the source COBOL to use UNIX files more efficiently.
- Make potential changes in database access, depending on the types of databases involved.
- Use some means of simulating transaction processing on UNIX (some tools are described later in this chapter).

In general then, batch COBOL programs using relational or VSAM files can be economically converted to UNIX. The result will not be as efficient as a new design but will move the system and will require a minimum of personnel retraining. Notably these procedures will not result in an efficient client/server environment without considerable redesign.

9.3   CICS

The following products provide CICS capabilities on UNIX: UNIKIX from Integris (a BULL company) and CICS/6000 from IBM. CICS/6000 is described in a later section.

UNIKIX provides the following services on a single platform:

- Direct translation of existing COBOL CICS programs to UNIX, including all essential functionality of CICS.
- A VSAM product that provides all VSAM services as used by CICS.
- Utilities to move VSAM data from MVS to UNIX.
- Simulated 3270 type terminal emulation for most "dumb" terminal types.
- Direct translation of screen panels defined with CICS basic mapping service (BMS).

UNIKIX uses a precompiler to generate standard COBOL for the CICS statements. A Microfocus COBOL compiler is used to generate executable code from the output of the precompiler. This method allows use of embedded SQL from most popular database vendors by using the database vendor–supplied SQL precompiler first and then the UNIKIX precompiler. UNIKIX provides utilities to handle embedded SQL for Oracle and Informix to improve efficiency.

Both UNIKIX and CICS/6000 are useful for moving COBOL CICS applications to UNIX (CICS/6000 is available for IBM's AIX) where the application will run on a single platform using old-style terminals (or a work station with software that can simulate them). UNIKIX does not have the capability of distributing transactions at this time, although the company states that it will develop this capability if requested.

9.4   CICS/6000

CICS/6000 is a robust product from IBM that runs on IBM's AIX operating system. AIX is a POSIX and XPG3 (X/Open operating system specification) compliant, UNIX-type operating system. For the purposes of this book, it can be considered UNIX, though it is slightly different in some respects. AIX is the operating system used on the RISC System/6000 computer.

There is some debate about whether CICS systems should be called a client/server product; in many respects, though, CICS performs functions required for implementing enhanced client/server systems. CICS/6000 is included here not only because it provides a migration path for current CICS users but also because it is specifically designed to function in an open system environment with distributed computing capabilities, including client/server.

CICS/6000 features include:

- Complete compatibility with CICS on MVS and several other platforms.
- Advanced Program-to-Program Communications (APPC) via LU6.2 and TCP/IP.
- Full distributed transaction management, with excellent recovery capabilities.
- Support for COBOL and C programming languages.
- Interfaces for a number of relational and hierarchical databases, including support for the X/Open XA interface.
- Source compatibility with existing CICS applications.
- Support for a wide range of terminal types, including work stations, block mode terminals, and ATMs.

These features provide the flexibility to support enhanced client/server architectures using platforms including AIX, OS/2, MVS, and AS/400.

CICS/6000 for those currently using CICS has these advantages:

- Minimal retraining of personnel is necessary.
- Applications can be moved from platform to platform by recompiling source.
- Existing terminals can be gradually replaced with powerful work stations using the Motif (GUI) without affecting the basic system.

10

Security in the Client/Server Environment

As client/server techniques become more prevalent, many people are looking at the various security products available. This chapter explores the mechanism of security in the client/server environment with the intent of discussing how security *ought* to work, not necessarily how any product, functions.

This chapter is based on the Kerberos system developed at MIT, and some of it is derived, copied, or paraphrased from the paper "Kerberos: An Authentication Service for Open Network Systems" by Jennifer G. Steiner, Clifford Neuman, and Jeffrey I. Schiller (1988). The chapter leaves out some material in the interest of simplifying the subject, most notably, encryption methods. Also, in order to present the basic operation of the system, not all potential breach points have been fully discussed.

10.1 OVERVIEW

The basic purpose of security is to prevent unauthorized access to proprietary data and computer services for any purpose. To provide maximum security, the enterprise must:

- Protect against physical access to terminals, work stations, servers, and the physical communication devices that connect them.
- Limit usage by authorized personnel to those functions which required to perform their duties.
- Protect against techniques that allow retrieval of messages in the network without physical entrance to the premises.
- Protect against tampering with the network so that personnel cannot redirect messages.

This chapter will discuss how software can be used to protect against improper usage by people who are authorized to use the system and provide some protection against long-distance pickup and network tampering. Long-distance pickup is a process made possible by modern electronics, which allows deciphering the electronic pulses on a wire from a distance. Fiber optic technology has reduced the capability for long-distance tapping but has not completely eliminated it. Not all systems have all the features described here, and some systems may have features not described. The techniques are provided as illustrations and are derived from Kerberos, but the descriptions do not necessarily reflect accurately the details of how that system functions.

10.2   SPECIAL SECURITY CONSIDERATIONS

10.2.1 General Discussion

Some companies find that the usual sign-on requirements when accompanied with intelligent distribution of access privileges provide sufficient security. Generally these simpler security provisions provide protection only against accidental mistake. It is still true that most security approaches, and certainly the more common ones, can be breached by anyone with sufficient determination and knowledge.

When there is only one computer, such as a mainframe, sign-on procedures coupled with physical access security are quite sufficient (except for the military, of course, but that is another matter entirely). With the advent of the client/server and access to systems more difficult to control, far more stringent and complex security requirements are raised.

10.2.2 Network Security Requirements

Network security is the first line of defense against unauthorized access. The network must also be protected against physical hazard and tapping. Network security requirements, then, include:

- Protection against physical access where the network could be physically harmed or tapped.
- Protection against access that may provide unauthorized modification or retrieval of data.
- Protection against access that could result in unauthorized use of enterprise computing resources.
- Protection against advanced techniques that allow tapping from a distance,

In addition to password security, the network can be protected by:

- Prevention of access to network equipment and wiring by unauthorized personnel, including preventing people from getting into locations where network facilities are placed.
- Double password techniques, whereby a single user must enter two passwords or two different people must enter passwords to get access.
- Encryption of data placed on the network so that even if the network is tapped, the data cannot be easily interpreted.
- Close monitoring, by personnel and by software, of system usage to detect attempts at unauthorized use of enterprise resources.
- Security management policies that prevent the person assigning passwords from accessing services on the network. This is the rule most often violated.

10.3 CLIENT/SERVER SECURITY REQUIREMENTS

The security requirements in a client/server environment can be summarized by the following points:

- The security system must have a minimal impact on the user.
- It must have minimal effect on performance.

- Administration itself should be secure and not overly difficult.
- The security system must protect against:
  — Unauthorized usage of information in the system.
  — Access to individual servers (software and hardware) so that individuals can use what they need for their assigned efforts but nothing else.
  — Usage of passwords or other access to key information even if picked up remotely from the network.
  — Tinkering that would allow replacing a proper server with the tinkerer's special self-purpose server.
- The security system should allow associating users with certain client addresses, preventing entry from any other locations.
- The system must allow the enterprise to set a policy limiting users to a single session at a time but retain sufficient flexibility to allow the enterprise to use multiple simultaneous sessions by the selected users when required.

A user should need to sign on to the system only once per session. Once signed on, the user should not be aware that the security system is present.

Checking security will have some effect on performance, and the objective is to minimize that effect as much as possible. The use of tickets, (described later) provides a means to perform the time-consuming security operations once at the beginning of the session.

A security system should provide tools to make administration as simple as possible while retaining protection of security information. Passwords, and the ability to update privilege lists are particularly vulnerable to misuse and must be well protected.

Most of the items listed as requiring protection are obvious. Not so obvious is the need to protect against substitution of servers. Suppose that the user is printing out a proposal that the company would not like to fall into the hands of a competitor. Suppose that normally the printout will be directed to the printer server in a secure location. Now suppose an unscrupulous person attaches a server to the network such that the printouts going to the secure server also go to his or her server. That person can now receive copies of the proposal without the user's being aware of it. The security system must protect against this situation.

Good security practice allows only one simultaneous session per user. In some situations, this is not practical. One large company provides multiple work stations to its customer representatives, and they use them to work multiple customers or to access multiple databases at the same time for the same customer. Also when windowing systems are used, the application and the security system treat each window as a separate session. In these cases, multiple sessions are required. If multiple sessions are allowed, the system should be able to limit the sessions to specific client addresses and also provide for limiting the number of sessions by the same user.

10.4   HOW IT LOOKS

10.4.1 How the User Sees Security

The security administrator assigns a password to the user when the user is set up for access. The password assigned is a one-time-only password that must be changed by the user upon first entry into the system. Until the password is changed, the user has no access to any data or services in the system.

The system will ask the user for a new password at the first sign-on. Since the user's password is known only to the user, even the administrator cannot access the system with that user's ID. From the point that the user has validly signed on, the user will not need to be aware of the security system until the next sign-on.

10.4.2 How the Administrator Sees Security

The security administrator uses interactive tools to provide user identification and access to services. The administrator inputs several sets of information to the security system: a list of users, a list of the work stations in the system, a list of services, and a set of *access groups*. Each of these sets includes associated information.

The information in the list of users includes the user ID, the user password, and the access groups the user belongs to. Optionally, the user list may include information about the user such as full name, telephone number, and the work stations the user has authority to use. The list of work stations is actually a list of valid network addresses and the name of the security client for each address.

The list of services includes the name of the service and the access groups and/or users that may access the service.

An access group supports a means of grouping users by access privileges. Each member of the access group set contains (in this simplified description) a list of services that members of the group can access. Grouping services is also possible, and for administrative ease, this may also be done in large systems. When later discussions say that the system "knows" about something, it means that the system searches one or more of these lists and finds a satisfactory answer.

10.4.3 How the Application Programmer Sees Security

Ideally, the application programmer should not be aware of security at all. There are certain situations in which application programs may need to use the security services for additional application-specific security. Also, some client/server systems do not lend themselves easily to hiding security fully from the application programmer. Therefore, depending on the specific situation, the application programmer may:

- Include a function call on first entry into the application service that performs the security operation for the service.
- Use a function provided by the security system to obtain user information for application-specific security checks.

10.4.4 Checking Security in Programs

Security checks are sometimes included in programs because the available security system does not provide the specific checks required. For instance, when certain users can access only certain data elements (such as restricting access to the payroll values), few security systems can be found that provide such features. As long as the use of program security checking is limited to finer granularity than the overall security system provides, there is a minimum of harm that can be done, with the minimum determined by the overall security of the system.

It is relatively easy to modify either the source or the executable code of programs, so that unless programs are themselves secure (both source and executables), it is very likely that some unauthorized person will find a way to access restricted information. It is almost impossible to detect such a breach until after harm is done since the person is trusted to enter the system.

10.5   HOW IT WORKS

10.5.1 Authentication

Security begins with *authentication*. When the user wants to use a work station, only one piece of information can prove her or his identity: the user's password. From the user's viewpoint, logging into a client/server security system is the same as logging into a single machine, but the operation underneath is vastly different.

The security system is itself a client/server system. The security client is the local part of the security system that interacts between local security operations and the security services, which reside on a security master server. The rest of this discussion will call the local security part the client and will name each of the security services.

The user is prompted for a user name by the security client. Once it has been entered, a request containing the user's name and the name of a special service, known as the *ticket-granting service*, is sent to the authentication service, which checks that it knows about the client. If so, it generates a random session key that will be used between the client and the security ticket–granting service It then creates a ticket for the ticket-granting service that contains the client's name, the name of the ticket-granting service, the current time, a lifetime for the ticket, the client's network address, the authorization groups the user belongs to, and the random session key just created. This is all encrypted in a key known only to the ticket-granting service and the authentication service.

The authentication service then sends the ticket, with a copy

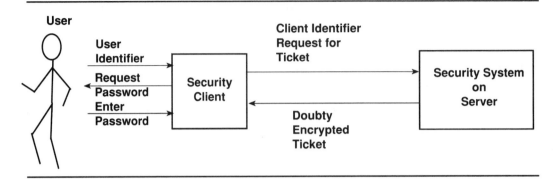

Figure 10.1   Authentication.

of the random session key and some additional information, back to the client. This response is encrypted in the client's private key, known only to the security system and the client, and is derived from the user's password. (See Figure 10.1.) When the client receives the response, it asks the user for a password. The password is used to decrypt the response from the authentication service. The ticket and the session key, along with some of the other information, are stored for future use, and the user's password is erased from memory.

Once the exchange has been completed, the work station possesses information that the security client can use to prove the identity of its user for the lifetime of the ticket-granting ticket.

10.5.2 Authorization

The authorization process checks that the user has the privilege of using the requested service and that the service is the one the user requested, not an unauthorized substitution.

To gain access to a service, the application first requests a ticket from the security client. If this is the first time the application has requested a ticket for this particular service, the security client requests the ticket from the security ticket–granting service. The security client passes the ticket to the application client and stores the ticket for the life of the session, so that it can return it to the application client without the overhead of requesting it again.

The application client then builds an authenticator containing the ticket received, user's name, network address, access groups of which the user is a member, and the current time (Figure 10.2). The authenticator is encrypted using the session key that was received with the ticket for the service. The client then sends the authenticator and ticket to the requested service.

When the application service has received the authenticator and ticket, it invokes a security function, which uses the session key included in the ticket to decrypt the authenticator, comparing the information in the ticket with that in the authenticator, the network address from which the request was received, and the present time. If everything matches, the security function checks to see if the requested service belongs to one of the access groups authorized for the user. If everything still checks, the security function returns a success indication to the application service that allows the service to proceed.

To prevent re-use of tickets, the security system checks the time for each use of any service from a given user. Checking the time is a little tricky, because it is not possible to guarantee that the clocks of various machines match exactly. Therefore, security checks that the time is within an acceptable range and no ticket with the same time has been used by the same user.

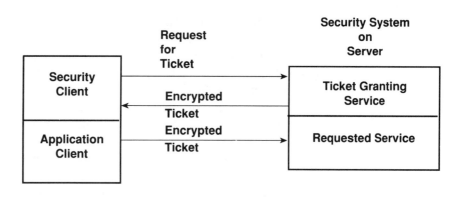

Figure 10.2   Authorization.

To verify its own identity, the application service adds one to the time stamp received, uses a security function to encrypt the result, and sends it back to the client.

At the end of this exchange, the application service is certain that, according to the security system, the user is who they say he or she says. If mutual authentication occurs, the application client is also convinced that the service is authentic. Moreover, the client and service share a key that no one else knows and can safely assume that a reasonably recent message encrypted in that key originated with the other party.

Service tickets must be obtained for each service the user wants to use. Tickets for individual services are obtained from the ticket-granting service, which works similarly to any other service in the system except that it is part of the security system.

10.6   SOME QUESTIONS TO ASK

Security is a large and complex subject. When the security of the data that supports an enterprise is concerned, it can also be the most important part of any system. Usually organizations do not pay much attention to security until there is a problem, probably because security is often looked at as an expensive frill. But as with any other investment, security must be examined with a cost-benefit lens:

- How much would it cost if the wrong people obtained proprietary enterprise information?
- How much would it cost if someone modified enterprise data (for instance, changing the values in accounts receivable)?
- What if someone were to destroy some or all of the enterprise information? Could the enterprise survive?
- What if someone inadvertently signed on to the wrong system and updated information without proper authority and, worse, proper knowledge?
- What is the possibility that any of these things could happen?

The potential of the costs mentioned must be weighed against the cost of security. Security costs include:

- Purchase of software security products
- Physical security costs
- Potential loss of system performance (especially if the security system is not properly designed)
- Cost of security administration
- Cost of monitoring the security system

A good security system will minimize its effect on performance. There may be some delay in sign-on or when a service is first used in the session, but thereafter the computing resources required by security are minimal (though never zero). If the current capacity of the system only marginally meets the performance requirements, then adding security may require more powerful hardware, including more communications capacity.

The cost of security administration can be minimal, especially considering the fact that most systems require some sort of user identification and sign-on already. If the system provides proper administration tools, it should cost little more to administer than what is already being done.

If the security system is not monitored regularly, it should not be used. Any good security system provides logs of attempts to enter by unauthorized people and it should provide a means to look at and analyze these logs. The logs contain many entries in which the user has simply made a mistake. The system will provide a tool to help identify repeat attempts and identify "hacking" for passwords, and such efforts.

10.7 A WORD ABOUT PASSWORDS

Passwords are the main line of defense against unauthorized access. Their management is a much-discussed topic, and there is much disagreement about exactly how to manage passwords. In a recent movie, a computer hacker gained access to the system by guessing that the system creator had a "back-door" entry, using a password easy to remember. It turned out that the professor had a grandson named Joshua (as does the author of this book), and the key password was therefore the grandson's name. Once the system was activated with this password, a lot of trouble followed.

Passwords like *Joshua* are therefore to be avoided. To prevent them, some systems place stringent rules on the formation of passwords, such as:

- The password must be different from the user identifier.
- No repeated characters are allowed.
- There must be at least one alphabetic and one numeric character in the password.
- There must be some minimum number of characters in the password (often six).

Some systems look the password up in a dictionary to prevent usage of personal names or real words.

The theory is that this type of password management will help prevent hacking into the system. Sometimes it does—and sometimes it does not. Consider the fact that the combination of not allowing repeated characters and requiring at least one alphabetic and one numeric character pretty much ensures that no actual word can be used. When these rules are used, the password becomes a meaningless set of characters and is difficult to remember. Many (too many!) people therefore write the password down and put it in a place that they deem secure. Thus is opened the door to a big breach. Passwords in the wallet, under the bookshelf, or under the pull-out of the desk do not protect the password, especially when the word is so obviously a password.

Password protection can be provided only by educating personnel on the importance of using a proper combination of characters. A telephone number is not okay nor are simple initials; perhaps using the initials of an acquaintance and the first and third digits of someone else's telephone number is okay.

11

Skill Requirements

We are in the midst of a revolution in computing. As networks become more useful and the price of networks and computers drops, the entire culture of developing systems is changing dramatically. Those who became accustomed to writing large, self-contained programs and systems designed to use a number of these large programs may find it difficult to encompass and accept the idea of developing small, single-function programs. New systems will be designed using these smaller, functionally oriented programs as building blocks for the formation of large, complex systems. This new culture is bringing:

- Elimination of purely batch-style programs and their associated JCLs.
- Special-purpose subsystems whose primary (perhaps only) function is to provide interactive graphical interfaces with the user.
- Substitution of on-line queries and presentation for printed reports, resulting in a dramatic decrease in the number of print programs and the amount of printed material produced.
- Expectation of very quick response to changing user requirements.

- Expectation of very quick response to user requirements for more data.
- A computer on every desk that can be as powerful as most mainframes have been.
- Continuation of the on-line data explosion, with data capacities in the terabytes becoming as common as megabytes were in the 1970s.
- Availability of vendor-provided application software that meets many needs and has the flexibility of variable functionality replacing the need for custom programs.
- Tools that allow the development of custom systems with greatly reduced effort.

Future skills requirements will change to match the change in the computing paradigm. There will be fewer programmers because users will be able to develop their own programs using the tools available. The simple business program will be developed less often, and technical expertise requirements for creating business applications will decrease. There will be a requirement for increased capability to create imaginative and highly technical products to make the computer a tool for the businessperson, the engineer, the scientist, and the individual.

As these changes take place, many programmers will become business analysts who make life easier for the rest of the business community by defining and developing tools. The more technically oriented will tend to become developers of the complex underlying systems that make the computer so easy to use, such as operating systems, object-oriented development tools, database management systems, and near-human language tools.

This chapter will address only one of the new areas where people will be required to change to match the technology: open distributed systems, lately called simply client/server technology.

11.1 THE CULTURE

UNIX has become the basis of the modern operating system. It has been established by both international standards and by industrial standards such as the X/Open XPG3. For many years UNIX was considered just another four-letter word by those in the mainstream of computing. But UNIX has emerged as the operating system of choice for modern computing. Other popular operating systems, such as MS-DOS, Windows, Windows/NT, and OS/2, have inherited many of the characteristics of UNIX. Whatever the flavor or the underlying technology, the culture represented by these operating systems is vastly different from the monolithic approach of the proprietary systems most computer users have been familiar with.

The new methods of client/server, with its entire spectrum of distributed computing, have an enormous impact on user's computer skills and attitudes. These must change a great deal to fit into the new methods. Some seemingly small changes have a large impact on the attitude of a person and the way a person works. The following changes are the crux:

- The average time to sign on to IBMs TSO, modify a program, and test it is about three minutes, not counting think time, compile time, or test execution time, but the average becomes less than ten seconds for any of the new operating systems.
- Creating a new DB2 database on MVS is at least a ten-step batch job and may take several minutes to complete after all data entry is finished. Creating a relational database on a modern system takes only two or three interactive steps, which are completed in less than a second after data entry is finished.
- New editors allow copying and moving program code from place to place with the click of a mouse button instead of the many steps previously required, and all operations respond in subsecond time, as opposed to the usual 10 to 20 seconds using mainframe editors.
- There are a large number of common utilities to search the system for information that did not exist on the mainframe, such as searching a set of files for values.
- New text editors which can check for many of the common programming mistakes without resorting to a compile (i.e., checking for balanced parentheses).

A new paradigm literally means an entirely new point of view, an entirely new framework for thought. So although these changes may appear to be merely improvements, they are the tips of the iceberg of change. These tools and the systems supporting them generate an entire realignment of responsibilities during system development. The time to develop a well-defined system has dropped from 50 percent of the total project to nearly 25 percent. Thus, the pure programmer is essentially gone into history, replaced by a computer specialist who must accept responsibility for at least portions of the design, rather than simply laying code.

Complicating the issue are some people who have been in the UNIX arena for a long time, including guru types who talk in terms meaningless to mainframe people or, worse, use the same words to mean different things. For instance, a *transaction processing system* to the mainframe is essentially a system that receives data and gives answers using terminals as opposed to batch jobs; a *transaction* to a mainframe person is a set of four letters that maps to a program. To an open systems person, however, a *transaction processing system* is any system that guarantees that either all work is done accurately or not done at all, and a *transaction* is a set of operations that must meet certain set criteria, such as transaction integrity.

More subtly, the computer becomes an immediate presence to the open systems developer. Old mainframes were always in the other room, and the operation of the development tools reinforced the feeling that the person was once removed from the computer. New systems, even though the server may be miles away, interface with the developer via a powerful computer, a work station, with tools that give the developer the sense of having a conversation with the computer.

Old systems would "bomb" a program. New systems "crash" the program. Old systems were unforgiving in everything; new systems can forgive much, but that puts more responsibilities on the developer to create proper programs.

Old systems required a large cadre of operators, systems programmers, special administrators, and others who had the privilege of modifying the system in certain ways. Some of these operations appear to exist with the new systems, but their function has changed so much that there is little comparison between the old and new for the actual effort or types of skills required. In many cases, the operator has been completely displaced by the user. A common expression to describe this phenomenon is to say that a lights out operation has replaced the glass house.

The use of distributed computing technology introduces its own complications to the new paradigm. Transaction processing was once considered a special requirement. Once there are two computers involved in any work, transaction processing becomes an absolute requirement, even though the systems used are not called transaction processing systems. The fact is that all applications always worked on transactions; however, nobody recognized that, unless they were trying to correct the data at four o'clock in the morning after a disk crash.

All client/server tools provide transaction management. Some provide it without mentioning it and others show it on the surface, but all must treat transactions atomically, or chaos is generated.

People who want to succeed in working with computers and managers who want successful computer systems need to come to grips with this new paradigm. They must change attitudes, change the focus of knowledge, and, most of all, change how they think of what is needed to become a successful computer professional.

11.2 JOB STRUCTURE

One of the benefits of the new computer platforms, and particularly client/server arrangements, is that the number of people required to service the basic system appears to decrease sharply. Two things can happen when management jumps to the conclusion that a client/server network does not require as many people as the old mainframe:

1. With insufficient and underskilled staffing, the system deteriorates, and the expected cost savings are wiped out by the cost of restoring the system and by lost user productivity.
2. Management does not understand the actual requirements and staffs the system as if it were the old mainframe, resulting in redundant personnel. Yet because of lack of relevant knowledge, the system deteriorates, and more costs are entailed in restoring the system and lost user productivity.

These situations may sound extreme, but they are exactly what has been happening. To correct the situation, management must realize that the new paradigm must replace the old. Some of the personnel requirements may seem similar, but in few instances is the actual type of work the same.

11.3 RECOMMENDATIONS

In general, there is a lower cost associated with the hardware and associated support software with the new systems. If management is not fully conversant with job needs, then they should use *People Rule 1: The ratio of the cost of system support personnel to the cost of hardware plus the cost of systems software is a constant.* In other words, if the enterprise has spent $1 million for hardware, operating systems, networks, and everything else, then it does not matter what type of system is used because the cost of support personnel will be the same. What actually happens is that when a company moves from the mainframe to client/server, the basic costs drop, and so do the support personnel costs, but they go down proportionately, not magically.

People Rule 1 always applies, but in the real world, there is some latitude, and knowledgeable managers can adjust the level of personnel to special situations. This is a sort of tuning effort and leads to: *People Rule 2: An ounce of understanding is worth ten pounds of memorized jargon.* This rule tells us that a person who understands how a system works, at its basic scientific level, will be far more effective than the person who memorizes reams of special terms but does not understand the scientific basis of the system. Of course, specific knowledge is always ultimately required, and part of the cost of personnel is paying them to learn, but memorization without understanding will not make a person effective in the system support role.

Using People Rule 2, management can select personnel who will be consistently effective and will maintain the level of system performance required without resorting to blindly hiring redundant personnel.

It is beyond the scope of this book to provide a complete compendium of personnel requirements and detailed qualifications.

The manager who must staff an open client/server environment will learn the real requirements for background and capability for each position. The next is a sort of corollary of the infamous Murphy's Law: *People Rule 3: Hiring by the letters has less chance of selecting qualified personnel than randomly picking from the résumé pile.* This rule states that sorting by the letters, such as looking in the résumé for mention of familiarity with UNIX, Oracle, Informix, TUXEDO, RS/6000, Pyramid, Novell Netware, SQL*Forms, CASE, or any other system will not, in and of itself, produce a proper selection. Look for capability first; then apply the cost of specific training and decide if the person is worth it.

The "looking for letters" approach has always been expensive, but as budgets tighten and senior management becomes less forgiving of high personnel costs, it becomes even more important to obtain staff who can understand what they are doing. Ultimately senior management will wonder why personnel costs remain so high when they have invested so much in the conversion to new systems, purportedly to save money and get better results.

11.4   TITLES AND POSITIONS

Titles and positions should be assigned by management, not by a book. Multiple jobs may be assigned to the same person or groups of persons. Here is a condensed list of functions with a very short description of each:

Business requirements definition

User requirements specification: Discover what the user wants and write it up, without regard to any technical effort required.

Data requirements specification: Analyze user requirements and develop the data elements and relationships required to satisfy those requirements.

Human factors engineering

Human interface design: Design the human interface for the proposed system. In modern computing, this is usually a specification of the GUI interface, essentially in user terms.

New design tools usage

Object-oriented design: Design the system in terms of objects, their relationships (including inheritance), and the operations required. All modern designs should be done using object-oriented techniques, no matter what language will be used to implement the system.

Database management

Database design: Design the database. This operation will translate the data specification to actual database definitions.

Database administration: Implement the database design. Define and implement database security. Ensure efficient physical database architecture.

New high-level language programming:

4GL programming: Implement the design using 4GL tools.

Object-oriented programming with high-level tools: Implement the design using object-oriented tools.

Hybrid, highly technical programming

C++ programming: Implement the design as objects using C++. This is a hybrid area, because there are many elements of C used in creating C++ programs.

GUI technical design and programming: Design the GUI interface to the human factors specification and implement it with the chosen language.

Third generation programming

C programming: Implement the design using C.

COBOL programming: Implement the design using COBOL.

New technology administration

Operating system administration: Define operating system parameters, install an operating system when required, and consult with application development personnel.

Client/server administration: Define client/server system, manage server location assignments, manage server loading, analyze statistics, and maximize system performance.

Network management

Network administration: Define the network, manage network security, and manage all aspects of data transport on the network.

Security administration: Define the security requirements, monitor security logs, review security procedures, assign privileges, and monitor all security arrangements.

Creating user and data requirements is the same function as in the past, but in a networked environment, with the larger databases and expectation of lower cost, they become critical functions.

People expect the computer to be an easy-to-use tool, with lots of navigation aids, using simple mouse clicks and function keys to make things happen. They expect that data entry requirements will be minimal and that the computer will help them to do their work simply and accurately. Human factors engineering has become an important factor in designing highly useful powerful systems.

Object-oriented design and object-oriented development tools are the methods of the future. As long as the resultant systems provide the basic performance and price/performance levels required, they should be used. In the future, people will be required to use these types of tools almost exclusively. Computer assisted software engineering (CASE) tools will become more prevalent, and CASE tools work best when the system is considered in terms of objects.

Programming with the various third-generation languages will proceed as in the past but with better editors and debugging tools. C++ will not only be a new language to the traditional programmer, but the techniques are extremely different, since they are object oriented. Programmers will need to learn how to define objects, how to define operations between objects, and how to replace the concept of structured code with the concept of objectivized code.

All of the administration functions change in substance and detail from their mainframe equivalents. Data movement over the network using the network protocol (such as TCP/IP and SPX) is sharply separated from the use of the data and transaction management. For instance, LU6.2 performs a mix of data movement and transaction management, whereas TCP/IP and other LAN and WAN protocols are limited exclusively to moving data between points. Network administration in the modern sense includes providing secure access to various nodes on the network, ensuring that there are alternate paths in case of emergency, and so forth. Often network administration includes administration of basic file server capabilities.

Client/server administration is a new function related to network management only in that the tools will use the network. For databases, the database administrator usually also manages the client/server by placing the proper databases on the server platforms, providing for connections from work stations, and so forth.

When the system is using enhanced client/server technology, the client/server administrator plans server placement, manages the distribution of servers, makes changes in server assignment, and performs other tasks to maintain performance and accessibility in the application.

Client/server administration is application oriented, and individuals may be assigned to administer specific applications. Network administration is oriented toward making computing platforms available to all users, and individual network administrators may be assigned to maintaining certain parts of the network, independent of the applications.

11.5   A WORD ABOUT POSITION HIERARCHIES

Providing job titles is difficult because client/server, and indeed all other open systems situations, are used in operations with from two small computers to the very largest with tens of servers and hundreds, or perhaps thousands, of work stations. The following hierarchy seems to be developing, but there has not been sufficient time to see how it all falls out. The hierarchy assumes at least one individual for each function within the management information serviced (MIS) department. The user must be involved intimately in all systems development, beginning with the creation of specifications and throughout the entire life of the system.

Note that the user may provide the personnel for some of the functions, such as human engineering. The hierarchy shown here is one attempt to clarify and highlight the differences between what will be present with client/server systems and what has been traditional with mainframes:

MIS director or vice-president
— Manager, systems services
— Manager, development
— Manager, technical services
— Manager, customer interfaces
— Manager, quality

Manager, system services
— Hardware purchase and maintenance
— Operating system purchase, administration, and maintenance
— Network purchase, administration, and maintenance
— Client/server administration

Manager, development
— Application system definition and design
— Application system implementation
— Application system maintenance

Manager, technical services
— Research available platform and client/server software
— Research available development tools
— Provide technical support to other departments

Manager, customer interfaces
— Provide human engineering expertise
— Help desk
— User documentation

Manager, quality
— Testing services
— Quality procedures
— Quality procedure auditing

Security is not mentioned in this hierarchy because the placement of security will vary greatly by organization. In some enterprises, an overall security department will set policies and review all security measures. The actual implementation of security will be done within the MIS organization as an administrative function.

11.6 HOW PEOPLE SHOULD PREPARE FOR WORKING WITH CLIENT/SERVER

The type and amount of effort required for preparing to enter the client/server world will depend on an individual's experience and role in the organization. In general, those who are not technically oriented should plan to move into the business arena and help users define objectives and requirements, or perhaps to implement systems using high-level tools. Those who are more technically oriented can move into programming using C and C++. The administration of the system software is also a possibility. In any case, everyone who intends to work in this technology should:

- Read books such as this one to become acquainted with the technology at a high level.
- Read the trade magazines (some are mentioned in the Bibliography).
- Study in the chosen area.
- Attend classes in the chosen area if at all possible.

Those new to this technology should use existing knowledge and experience wisely, avoiding looking at the new methods through the outdated paradigm of current methods and being ready to look for the advantages and using the new tools fully. Much of what was done with the old systems was designed to overcome deficiencies in the tools and platforms. These same types of activities should not be expected in open systems. Surely new deficiencies (hopefully, minimal to the current effort) will appear—and new tools will come along to overcome them.

Finally, follow these guidelines:

- If there is a PC available, begin to use it for practice.
- If going into development, try to develop a system on the PC.

- Expect to exhibit a new attitude toward the completion effort; it should be much less than previously, because of the power of the new tools to automate many tasks.
- Talk to people already involved with the new stuff and pick up how they work.
- Learn the new terminology, and be sure to be exact about term definition.
- If working with old and new at the same time, compartmentalize thinking to prevent confusing term meanings between the two cultures.

12

Miscellaneous Topics

12.1 PICKING CLIENT/SERVER 4GL OR OBJECT ORIENTED TOOLS

Recently a large number of development tool vendors have begun to advertise that their product is "object oriented" and designed specifically for client/server development and production. All of these products appear good from a development viewpoint, but not all will generate a system that will support a given enterprise. Some of the claims being advertised are that the product will:

- Improve programmer productivity.
- Improve client/server performance.
- Enable applications to be moved from one database product to another without effort.
- Provide a database with a development tool "better" than the widely known and used database products.
- Move applications to another platform with no effort.

All of these products will improve programmer productivity as long as the product is capable of creating a system that meets the specifications of the end user. Most of the products can meet any functionality. Many can meet just about any presentation requirements. Some, however, have difficulty in producing the panels, screens, and other presentations that an imaginative user might require because their internal logic forces certain formats on the presentation.

The user must examine very closely all claims for performance:

- Does the product provide a means of generating executable code, rather than always running by interpreting the source?
- Does the product use multithreading servers internally?
- How does the product access the database?
- Where is application processing done—in the work station or in the server?
- How does the product handle distributed data?

If the product does not provide for any type of compiling the production version, performance will be slower compared to a C program of the same functionality—and by a large margin. Some products claim to compile into a production version, but the "compile" simply tokenizes (as we say in technical jargon) the source. Tokenizing is the first step in a compile, so this "half-compile" does speed the execution of the application, but its performance cannot reach anywhere near that of the equivalent C program. A few products create a true executable module, which runs nearly as fast as a C program. The only way to tell (if technical information is not available) is to find out what the comparison actually is with C.

Many of the client/server development tools use dedicated server programs to interface with the database. One product examined actually created a server process for every user. When the technical representatives were questioned about this, particularly for the UNIX server, their response was that the server process placed no load on the system unless it was actually being used. Apparently they did not understand the process of context switching in UNIX. Depending on the power of the server platform, the context switching can become a bottleneck somewhere between 20 and 200 users. In other words, there must be a very large computer to process context switching if the enterprise anticipates more than about 20 users without using multithreaded servers. This type of system, when coupled with a multithreaded server database, will degrade performance considerably if there are many users. Certainly this factor alone will prevent using this type of system for any large enterprise in which thousands of users might be signed on at the same time. Figure 12.1 shows how a single-threaded server from an object oriented tool relates to a multithreaded database.

Almost all of the development tools, especially those billed as 4GL or object oriented, use a form of dynamic SQL to access databases. A few have worked closely with the database vendor to provide more efficient interfaces. Using dynamic SQL will slow the system by forcing the database to parse and optimize every access every time.

All known development tools do their processing in the work station. Beyond that, they tend to send two to five times more SQL requests to the database than a well-written C program would. The result is a requirement for a more powerful work station, and if only a few users are present, the server tends to sit idle. Additionally, the network load increases even more than if using the database alone.

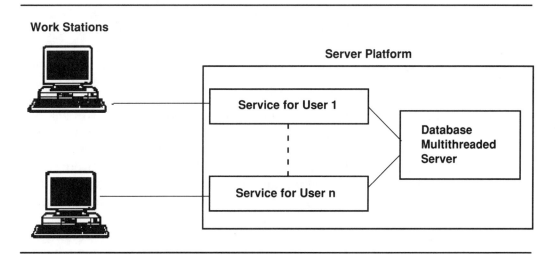

Figure 12.1   Single-threaded with Multithreaded Servers.

All of these products claim that they will work with multiple types of databases. Many claim that heterogeneous databases can be mixed in the same application. Usually these claims are true. The cost of this flexibility in these cases is loss of performance because they must make special provisions to accommodate multiple databases.

Many development tools provide a proprietary database with the development product, and the vendor recommends its use over other database products. By using its own database, the vendor can include special access capabilities to increase performance. The problem with using these databases is that they are usually not as mature and robust as databases from major vendors. Further, they usually cannot accommodate large volumes of data, in excess of a few gigabytes, in a single database.

Almost all of these products cannot handle distributed data within their own system but rely instead on the distribution capability of the underlying database. Obviously performance becomes limited by factors discussed in Chapter 5. Some object-oriented tools vendors claim they support distributed processing. Although they provide some sort of routing capability, none provides distributed transaction management. Without transaction management, *updates cannot be distributed.*

Some of the advertised products do, in fact, provide a pseudo-transaction management but with a loss of performance. Since they do not include a standard transactional interface, such as defined by the X/Open distributed transaction specification, they must rely on their own methods for implementing the equivalent of a two-phase commit. These products log every SQL update, and if any database commit fails, they use the log to back out update previously committed at the database level. Writing these logs require an extra write to disk for every SQL statement.

If the product does not support the use of advanced client/server software as a foundation, then its use becomes very limited.

The conclusion is that these products do provide many good capabilities but should be used only:

- When the system will serve a relatively small number of users.
- When the database is relatively small.

- When the system is relatively uncomplicated.
- For ad hoc query.

Every enterprise considering using existing 4GL or object-oriented products for development of a critical application must carefully analyze their requirements, especially performance and number of users, before committing to the product. They must look beyond the hype and pictures and determine if the product will generate a system that meets needs long enough into the future to amortize the development cost.

12.2 MORE ON WHERE TO PROCESS

There is a lot of discussion among software engineers about where application processing should occur: in the work station or in the server. Those who opt for processing in the work station point out that the purpose of the server is to support many users, so it most likely will not have the power to do much application processing. Those who recommend that application processing should be done in the server point out that network limitations are a severe bottleneck when processing in the work station and that this bottleneck usually leaves the server idle a large portion of the time. What is the right answer? There is not one. In previous chapters, many factors were pointed out. The following paragraphs provide a summary.

Most modern networks limit the number of users with work station application processing because of the need to carry large amounts of data on the line. This limit looms large for most business processes because they are data intensive; they require multiple accesses to the database to process the application. As networks become faster and cheaper, this limitation will gradually become less severe and less costly but can never go away altogether.

Processing in the work station is simpler because the application system can be treated as a single location system, just as in the good old days. This is especially true because of the many tools available to help develop this type of system.

If a large number of users, on the order of hundreds or thousands, use the system simultaneously, the network bottleneck forces the processing to be done in the server. Using the server merely as a database machine will often leave it idle because the network cannot deliver requests for data and then return the data fast enough to load the server (always assuming that the database uses multithreading and other efficient approaches).

What should an enterprise do? If the enterprise has access to staff who are aware of the alternatives, the technical issues involved, and the business needs of the enterprise, they should be relied on to ask the right questions and develop a system using the correct products to match user needs. But even the largest companies often do not have these types of staff available. Or, worse, the decisions are made by people of authority who do not ask the questions first. Nevertheless, any organization contemplating moving forward using systems based on client/server technology must get the answers before investing. Nontechnical decision makers must do the following:

- Become aware that there are multiple types of systems available, though it is not necessary to know all the technical aspects of each system.
- Determine the qualifications of advisory personnel, particularly their breadth of knowledge of the business and the technology available.
- Never pick anyone who has already determined the best solution.
- Never trust any vendor implicitly.
- Use independent consultants, even if recommended by a vendor (the most reliable vendors for these recommendations are the hardware platform vendors) as long as they pass the other tests.
- Examine the experience of other enterprises with the various types of solutions.

The decision maker should be thoroughly satisfied that the system will meet the business needs that have been determined. Otherwise he or she should look further or test the contemplated products thoroughly to prove their worth for the particular application.

No enterprise should reject use of consultants, products or platforms because they have been "burned." They should reexamine the selection criteria for people and products and find out how the previous poor decisions got through. It is easy to be mesmerized by slick presentations, so stick to the center of the matter.

One consultant was called by a major corporation to discuss use of client/server products for its particular application. The organization had already completed 90 percent of the development using monolithic, single-platform techniques, and then the question came up about how to convert to client/server. The consultant noted that the monolithic programs would require splitting into client and server processes to meet their needs correctly. The organization managers told the consultant that he did not know what he was talking about because they *knew* that they simply had to run their programs on the work station and the client/server arrangement would be done automatically. Of course, this can be done using only a database server, so their server platform would support about 50 users rather than the 500 they could support on the same server platform with a monolithic system. The alternative, using enhanced client/server technology, would have supported at least the required 500 users and would have also supported expansion much beyond that. The suggested solution was rejected out of hand.

Another enterprise rejected the use of enhanced client/server to build a 6000-plus user, high-performance system, but after two years of trying with the database server, they realized the need for something else and returned to the original consultant for help. Good planning and recognition of technical realities would have saved a lot of expense and bad public relations.

Appendix A

The Order Entry Application Requirements

A.1 OVERVIEW

A.1.1 The Company

The Nice Little Thing Company manufactures a line of Nice Little Things that people want. There are many types of Nice Little Things, each with a variety of features. The company sells via catalog to stores, both large and small, throughout the United States. Because of the popularity of Nice Little Things, the company has opened offices in Chicago, Dallas, Los Angeles, and Denver. The home office is still in the city where the concept of Nice Little Things began, Springfield, Missouri. There are two warehouses where shipments are made—one in Springfield at the home office and one in Los Angeles. The Los Angeles warehouse is not close to the Los Angeles office.

Total volume of Nice Little Things is very high, and since the price per unit is relatively low, the company must keep the cost of manufacture and distribution very low.

A.1.2 The Current Order Entry System

Orders come by mail and telephone to the branch offices, with some coming in to the home office. Orders are processed manually. Shipping forms are prepared, a list of bad credit risks is checked manually, and the orders are sent by messenger to the warehouse each day. Each office sends orders to an assigned warehouse. Only the warehouse employees know the level of stock within their warehouse. Stock is replaced by each warehouse by ordering from the Springfield manufacturing plant.

Each warehouse maintains a back order file, and when goods are received, shipments are made to fill back orders in a FIFO (first in–first out) order.

A computerized customer list and accounts receivable are maintained from copies of shipping orders sent to the home office daily. At the home office, a room full of entry clerks maintain the customer list and accounts receivable.

All receipts come to the home office. where they go to that same room full of entry clerks for posting.

A.1.3 What the Company Wants

The company wants to provide better service to its customers by developing the capability to provide information instantly on product availability when an order is received. At the same time, the company would like to provide instant status on all orders from any office. In addition, the company would like to check the customer accounts receivable status before an order is actually shipped without holding up any orders. Of course, the company would like to do this while cutting costs of order entry or increasing the number of orders that can be processed on any given day, or both. The company would also like to decrease the time between receipt of an order from a customer and the actual shipment.

The company wants to streamline the warehouse selection process so that if an item is available at any warehouse, it can be shipped from there. It is considering opening additional warehouses and wants the system to be capable of expanding to service the new warehouses without modification.

A.2   SPECIFIC REQUIREMENTS

A.2.1 What the Users Need

Orders received by telephone may be received and entered by clerks, secretaries, sales staff, managers, or anybody else who happens to answer the telephone. Orders received by mail will be entered by clerks specifically assigned to the task. In all cases, orders will be entered using a work station. The order entry system will:

- Present the user with an easy-to-use, mouse-driven, windows-oriented GUI that guides the user through the necessary steps.
- Respond immediately (subsecond response) to the user.
- Provide edits that will prevent the user from entering bad information. Edits will include validation of customer number, item identification (stock keeping unit (SKU) or item number), and other checks.
- Provide the ability to obtain customer number by entering the customer name, with transference of the customer number to the order by a single mouse click.
- Offer an option whereby the availability of each item will be tested as the item is entered, with immediate notification if the item is not available in sufficient quantities to satisfy the order.
- Give immediate pricing for each item as it is entered, with extension.
- If discounts are allowed, either by quantity or special discounts for a particular customer, automatically take them as each item is entered.
- Make available discount rules from a separate window, easily retrieved for either the customer or for a specific item.
- When the order has been completely entered, notify the user either that the order will be shipped or that it is held up for stock unavailable or for accounts receivable irregularities.
- Ask the system to ship anyway, leaving back orders.
- Override accounts receivable irregularities only by specifically authorized personnel.
- Determine the warehouse(s) from which the shipment will be made and the date of the shipment.
- Display order status on-line so that people can answer customer requests on status immediately.
- Access the corporate customer database and the old order database for use when talking with customers.

Clerks entering mail orders generally will not use or be aware of the order status, except that the order has been successfully entered. People entering telephone orders will be able to discuss the order status with the customer as the order is entered, providing instant response to requests.

A.2.2 System Capacity

Initially, three remote branch offices, one branch office at the home office, and the home office staff will use the system. There will be from 3 to 6 work stations at each branch office, and 25 work stations at the home office using the system, making a total of about 49 work stations signed on to the system during available hours. The staff estimates that about half of these will be active during most of the available hours, with all of them being active at peak hours (about two hours each workday).

The company handles about 1000 orders per day now, with about ten items per order, all from the home office, but wants the system to handle 2000 orders per day with ten items per order, all from the branch offices as soon as it goes on-line. In an eight-hour day, this implies that the system must handle about four orders per second. Considering the time differences among the branch offices, the peak load will be about three orders per second and dwindle from there. The company wants the system designed to handle the peak load without difficulty.

A.2.3 Performance

Response to user queries must be less than a second during normal peak load 99.5 percent of the time and 90 percent of the time during peak load. During order entry, the same requirement is placed on all activity required to build the order. When an order has been completed and is being processed, up to a two-second response will be acceptable.

Since the company business is a wholesale business, there is no perceived need for 24-hour, seven-day availability, although the company may want to increase availability in the future. For now, the system must be available from 9:00 A.M. Eastern Time to 6:00 P.M. Western Time or, from the home office point of view, 8:00 A.M. Central Time to 8:00 P.M. Central Time.

During the period of required availability, downtime can be

costly, since the company already receives a large percentage of orders over the telephone and intends to make instant response to these orders a major part of its marketing strategy. Downtime on the order of one hour per month or less is envisioned.

A.2.4 Data Integrity

The company wants a system that protects against corrupted data. The characteristics desired are:

- The databases must accurately represent the latest information at all times.
- In case of failure, procedures must provide rapid and accurate recovery.
- If the system fails while transactions are in process, the system must ensure that all incomplete transactions are backed out and information made available to reenter them accurately.
- Information from partial transactions must not enter the database or be available to anyone except the person working on the transaction.

A.2.5 Technical Requirements

Technical requirements include these:

- All users will work at work stations using Windows.
- All databases will be accessible from any work station in the system.
- The customer list will be common to all customer information systems, including mailing lists.
- All databases, including the inventory and accounts receivable, will be available to their respective subsystems, including the planned general ledger system.
- Inventory management will occur at the individual warehouses and at the home office.
- Accounts receivable will be updated at all branch offices and at the home office.
- Orders from any customer will be entered from any branch office and the home office.

- It must be possible to increase the capacity of the system by adding or replacing work stations and servers without program changes.
- Dependence on specific vendors and their products will be minimized.
- It must be possible to change the network (WAN and LAN) without program changes, or at the very least changes must be minimized and localized for minimum impact.
- Databases must be protected by backups.
- Database replication must be minimized.

A.2.6   Cost Requirements

Cost requirements are flexible but must be controlled. Increased development cost may be acceptable if the benefits in flexibility and performance warrant them. The cost of administration must be kept as low as possible, requiring administrative effort only during initial set-up and to accommodate changes in platforms or to fine-tune the system as it matures.

Cost of maintenance to programs must be limited to those required for changing system features. Use of 4GLs and object-oriented development tools will be encouraged where performance and future flexibility are not unduly compromised.

In any case, costs will be estimated before purchase decisions are made. The company expects that the cost for development and maintenance will be accurately estimated. Cost overruns are not tolerated.

A.2.7   Development Schedule

The development schedule must be aggressive. Costs and schedule considerations will be considered together. The schedule, once established, will be adhered to. Surprises from technical or performance happenings will not be acceptable.

Appendix B

The Network
for Order Entry

B.1   TYPE OF NETWORK

B.1.1   The Local Area Networks

Each branch office and the home office use LANs. The home office network is a high-speed LAN with a bandwidth of 10 Mb. The home office is wired to support this LAN with outlets in each office.

The company has not chosen a vendor yet. Cost will be the paramount consideration in choosing the vendor, along with the reliability, future expansion, and other considerations.

B.1.2   The Wide Area Network

The cost of a WAN increases dramatically with bandwidth. The company hopes to use a relatively low-cost WAN with a bandwidth of 56 Kb. The company expects to make arrangements with its normal communications vendor for the WAN connections.

B.1.3   The Protocol

After examining the confusion surrounding the protocols and much soul searching, the company has decided to use TCP/IP protocol throughout the network. TCP/IP has the advantage of being available on all network products and all operating systems. It is also widely used, providing a pool of experienced network administrators in the job arena.

The company is also looking at using LAN supplier protocols, such as Netware IPX/SPX or NetBIOS, for some applications in the home office.

B.2   THE NETWORK ARCHITECTURE

B.2.1   Overview

Figure B.1 illustrates the system logical network. Each branch office has a server and a number of work stations. A larger server for containing master databases and company records will be

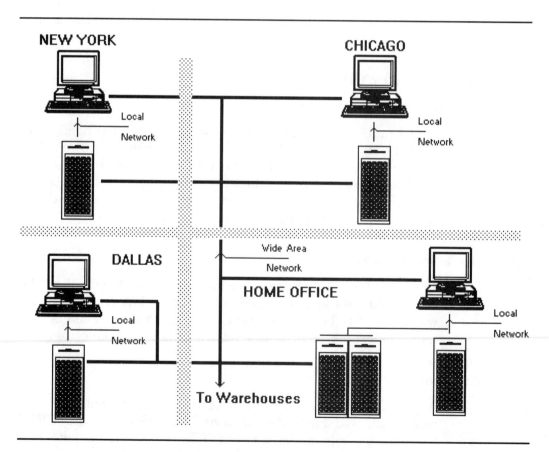

Figure B.1   System architecture.

placed at the home office. There is a branch office physically located in the home building, which will have its own server. As the company grows, more servers may be added at the branch office.

The branch offices are connected to each other and the home office with a WAN. There is an LAN at each branch office and at the home office.

The architecture as shown here is the logical look (it does not show the physical wiring, concentrators, routers, etc.). One important aspect of this architecture is that a message from any platform can reach any other platform in the system with a single logical hop.

The warehouses also have networks to support their local requirements. The order entry system requires only that the information from the orders be delivered accurately to the warehouse system and that shipment status be returned to the order entry system. This will occur via the WAN.

B.2.2 The Branch Office Networks

The configuration of the branch office networks is illustrated in Figure B.2. The application programs are initiated on Windows work stations. The local server may be an MS-DOS or UNIX system, depending on the decision of the system developers.

The company is expecting to maintain local databases at each branch office to provide the fastest response. These databases will contain information most likely to be required at the branch office. Since any branch office may receive orders from anyone, the branch office must be connected to all other branch offices and the home office to access parts of the database that may not be stored locally.

B.2.3 The Home Office Network

The branch office at the home office location will be the same as at other branch offices (Figure B.2), except that it will be connected to the home office LAN instead of to the WAN. The home office configuration is illustrated in Figure B.3.

The corporate central server will manage the corporate database, which consists primarily of the master customer list, the accounting information, and management information systems.

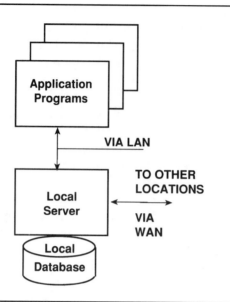

Figure B.2   Branch office configuration.

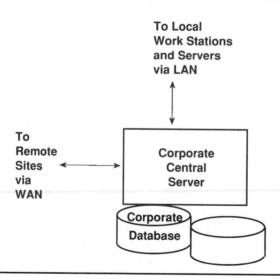

Figure B.3   Home office configuration.

The corporate database will also contain closed order information for all orders closed more than a month. The company hopes it will be able to maintain at least two years of information on orders for use in analysis.

B.3 NETWORK BANDWIDTH

The cost of LANs is reasonable for 10 Mb at each branch office and at the home office. There will be very little activity on the branch office LANs except for the order entry system. The home office LAN must also support development and other systems. It is reasonable to assume that the home office LAN can handle 5 Mb of traffic for the order entry system.

The cost of WANs is relatively high. It is most likely that the widest bandwidth the company will be able to afford at this time is 56 Kb, with 112 Kb possible if business expands as expected. (Note that Mb is "million bits per second" and Kb is "thousand bits per second." Thus, the 10 Mb LAN can handle 1.25 million bytes per second, and the 56 Kb WAN can handle 8000 bytes per second.)

When designing the system, it is accepted practice to design for a maximum of 75 percent of planned bandwidth to allow for instantaneous peak loads.

Appendix C

A Brief Overview of Open Systems Standards

There are two types of standards: those written by a recognized standards body and de facto standards that recognize the reality that everyone uses a certain convention. This appendix will discuss only written standards. It will present a quick description of some of the standards and their history.

C.1 STANDARDS FROM INTERNATIONAL STANDARDS ORGANIZATION (ISO)

C.1.1 ISO Open Systems Interconnect (OSI) Reference Model

ISO-OSI is referenced by all people working with networks. This is the well known seven layer model:

Application
Presentation
Session
Transport
Network
Data Link
Physical

Information flows up from the physical media (coaxial, twisted pair, microwave, etc.) and down from the application layer. The application layer is not necessarily the actual application as seen by the end user but includes anything that receives the information from the network, such as a database or a system like TUXEDO.

The presentation layer provides services that prepare the data and present them to the application layer. It does not have anything to do with presenting the information to people.

The rest of the layers manage the transmission of information to ensure that what is received is exactly what was sent.

TCP/IP provides everything from the transport layer down. Most current networking systems do not include an active presentation or session layer.

LU6.2 provides the equivalent of all layers, including the application layer. UNIX offers a transport layer interface (TLI) that provides a sort of presentation layer and isolates the application layer from the lower layers. Using TLI, an application layer system can be connected with any networking system that provides a transport layer without regard for the underlying networking system.

C.1.2 ISO Distributed Transaction Processing

The ISO standard *Information Processing Systems–Open Systems Interconnection–Distributed Processing* is a high-level standard for distributed transaction systems. It includes a standard model, a set of protocols, and a set of services. No API is included; others, such as X/Open, are creating the APIs. The ISO distributed processing standard is placed in the application layer.

C.1.3 ISO Two-Phase Commit

The ISO standard *Information Processing Systems-Open Systems Interconnection–Service Definition for the Commitment, Concurrency, and Recovery Service Element (CCR)* includes an application layer standard for two-phase commit and recovery capability. Again, no API is provided, just a protocol and capability definition. The ISO CCR has been implemented by most database vendors and is a required integral part of all distributed transaction processing systems.

C.2   IEEE-POSIX

IEEE (Institute of Electric and Electronic Engineers) has received a charter from both ISO and ANSI (American National Standards Institute) to develop an open, standard operating system API. Several standards have been published, and most UNIX-type operating systems have been certified POSIX compliance. These standards provide an API for providing operating systems services. They do not provide any hint about implementation.

Microsoft expects to get Windows/NT certified POSIX compliant.

C.3   X/OPEN DISTRIBUTED TRANSACTION PROCESSING SPECIFICATIONS

X/Open Company is an independent, worldwide, open systems organization supported by most of the world's largest information systems suppliers, user organizations, and software companies. It provides specifications to support open systems, and these specifications become de facto standards to most enterprises.

The document *Distributed Transaction Processing: The XA Specification,* published by X/Open, is the first of several specifications relating directly to distributed processing and client/server processing. This specification defines the distributed transaction model and the API for the interface between the transaction manager and resource managers.

Future specifications from X/Open are expected to define:

- An API providing the capability of transaction start and stop (transaction demarcation) for the application program.
- An API to support peer-to-peer distributed and cooperative computing.
- An expanded XA specification, sometimes called XA+.

C.4   OPEN SOFTWARE FOUNDATION

The Open Software Foundation (OSF) was formed to develop open systems platforms. It is supported by many major information systems vendors. OSF develops and sells open systems products to its members. For distributed processing and client/server, OSF provides the distributed computing environment (DCE), which provides many services required for these environments. Because OSF DCE is being used or considered by many users, it is becoming another de facto standard.

OSF also provides Motif, a GUI based on X/Windows.

C.5   UNIX INTERNATIONAL

UNIX International is an organization of UNIX users and vendors of UNIX products. UNIX International traditionally has suggested specifications to UNIX System Laboratories for features desired for UNIX and related products. UNIX International has developed a specification for a distributed computing environment, UI-ATLAS. It has also provided a document, *Requirements for Transaction Processing*, which recognizes the need for full transaction processing capabilities in the client/server environment. Work from UNIX International is not considered to set standards, but because of the importance of the membership, the work tends to find its way into standards and standards compliant products. Those working with client/server should be aware of this organization and its work.

Appendix D

A Short Discussion of Two-Phase Commit

This brief discussion provides only a general overview of the subject. Actual recovery methods, a full discussion of the implications when there is a failure, and other details would require much more space. The discussion actually describes the form of two-phase commit known as *presumed abort*, which has become standard. (See the bibliography for more information about two-phase commit.)

Figure D.1 shows the sequence of events during a two-phase commit operation. The commit process begins with a call by the application to commit the transaction. When the transaction manager receives the commit request (assuming that there are no problems) the sequence is as follows:

1. The transaction manager sends a vote request to each resource manager, in this case, database 1 and database 2.
2. Database 2 may send its vote first; in this case it votes okay.
3. Database 1 sends an okay vote.
4. When the transaction manager has received votes from all resource managers, it analyzes them. In this case all are okay, so it sends a final commit message to all resource managers.
5. Databases 1 and 2 complete the request process and return a message indicating that the commit was successful.

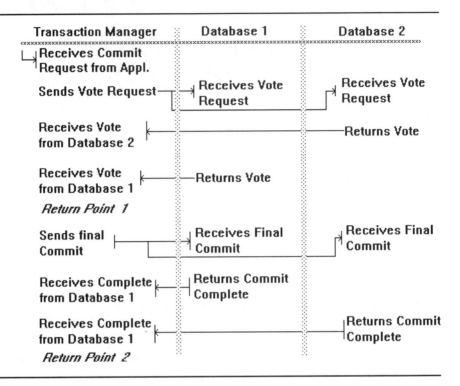

Figure D.1   Two-phase commit sequence.

6. The transaction manager returns a commit okay message to the application when it is sure that all commits are complete.

The most secure time to respond to the application is when the transaction manager has received good responses for a final commit from all resource managers (Return Point 2 in the diagram). For faster response, the transaction manager may return to the application at Return Point 1, after all votes have been received.

There are some important terms to be familiar with:

- A transaction is *in-flight* until the transaction manager has sent the vote request to all resource managers.

- A transaction is *in-doubt* between the time the transaction manager requests votes and the time it has received responses from all resource managers.
- A transaction is *complete* when the transaction manager has received a final commit completion message from all resource managers or when it has decided to abort the transaction.
- *Abort*, sometimes called *rollback*, means to remove all effects of the transaction from the resource, usually a database.
- The vote request is sometimes called *prepare*.

Each resource manager will consider the transaction in-doubt after receiving a vote request until it has received either a commit or abort (rollback) request from the transaction manager.

There is not space here to explain fully the recovery procedures used after a failure when using two-phase commit. The following points are important:

- The transaction manager will send a final commit request to the transaction managers only if it receives all okay responses to the vote requests. Otherwise it will send abort requests to all resource managers.
- Resource managers are free to abort their portion of the transaction at any time before they receive a vote request.
- Once a resource manager has responded OK to a vote request, it must remain ready to commit or abort the transaction on request from the transaction manager, under any circumstances, including a complete platform failure (after the system has resumed operation).
- If the transaction manager does not receive a response from a resource manager to a vote request, it may assume that the resource manager has already aborted or will abort the transaction—hence the term *presumed abort*.
- Once the transaction has reached the in-doubt state, recovery is guaranteed to abort or commit the entire transaction, unless a resource manager has unilaterally committed or aborted.

Transaction managers will make an option available when there is a need (particularly in case there is a massive, long-term failure) to complete transactions on individual resource managers. When the recovery procedures are run, the transaction manager will analyze the situation and will inform the user whether transaction integrity has been breached.

Since two phase-commit requires several interactions between the transaction manager and the resource managers, two optimizations are usually provided:

- The transaction manager will not invoke two-phase commit unless more than one resource manager was involved in a transaction, instead sending a *vote-commit now* request to the single resource manager, thus using only one interchange to complete the commit.
- A resource manage may have information that no updates were processed by it and will in this case send an *OK complete* return to a vote request, thus causing the transaction manager not to send any further messages to the resource manager for this transaction.

Some transaction managers will send a vote request to all but one of the resource managers, and if all vote okay, it then sends a vote-commit request to the remaining resource manager. Depending on the response from that resource manager, the transaction manager will send either a commit or abort request to the rest of the resource managers. This optimization saves one interchange.

If the transaction manager receives all vote-complete responses, it will send no more messages to the resource managers. If the system designer knows this will always be the case, then the application should not invoke the transaction manager at all for transaction beginning or completion.

At two points, the transaction manager can respond to the application that the transaction has been completed. Return Point 1 will always be used if the transaction manager has decided to abort the transaction. If Return Point 1 is used when the transaction manager will (eventually) commit the transaction, it may improve the performance of the system but leaves the problem that there could be a system failure before the resource managers have actually committed the transaction. Since the good response to the application will probably cause the application to continue with the assumption that the transaction is fully committed, the application could get into trouble. Normally this cannot cause a loss of transaction integrity, but could cause a loss of information to the user for recovery purposes.

Glossary

This glossary defines some of the important terms peculiar to client/server and distributed processing. This book is written with the assumption that the reader is familiar with the common terms used in the information processing industry, so they are not included here. All definitions are made in the context of software systems. Many have more general meanings.

abort To cease a process and remove all interim affects of the process. If a transaction has updated a database and is then aborted, the database is restored to exactly the state it was in before the start of the transaction. Abort is sometimes called *rollback*.

ACID properties Transaction processing standards define a transaction by requiring that any processing must meet the ACID properties to be called a transaction. The ACID properties are as follows:

Atomicity: Each transaction is a complete entity; that is, all the work is either done or not done.

Consistency: Any changes to the system that remain at the end of the transaction must be consistent with the rules of processing. Changes made to a database must be consistent with the rules within the database. Consistency implies that every time the same information is processed, the result will be the same.

Isolation: Changes made by a transaction are not affected by changes made by any other transaction running at the same time. Isolation implies that changes made during the processing of a transaction are not seen by any other transaction until the first transaction commits.

Durability: All changes made during a transaction become persistent once the transaction commits. This means that once a transaction commits, changes made to a database must remain until further changes are made by another transaction.

advanced program-to-program Communications (APPC) A peer-to-peer protocol that provides full two-way communications between programs. APPC is supported via IBM's LU6.2 network communications system.

atomic In the general sense, the smallest possible object; in a more mathematical sense, a process or object complete in itself. An atomic object may be broken down into smaller pieces under certain circumstances, but its completeness may never be compromised. A transaction is atomic in the sense that it must be either all completed or all effects of its interim operations must be erased.

authentication The security process that verifies that the person using the system is who he or she says. Includes checking passwords and preparing the system for secure use.

authorization The security process that ensures that users have access only to the data and processes they are supposed to. Authorization includes granting privileges to users. For instance, a user may have the privilege of reading but not updating certain data.

bandwidth The amount of information that can be sent over a network in a given amount of time. The term is defined from the fact that as more information is put on the line in a given amount of time, it requires a wider frequency handling capacity, or bandwidth. Higher bandwidths carry more information than lower bandwidths.

baud A measure of the bandwidth in terms of the amount of information that can be sent. In this book and in most applications in the 1990s, *baud* is used to mean *bit rate*, though it has not always meant exactly that. For example, a 9600 baud modem has the capacity to transmit 9600 bits per second.

bit rate A measure of the bandwidth in terms of the number of bits that can be sent in a second. WANs can have as little bandwidth as 56,000 bits per second, written 56 Kb. LANs often have a bandwidth capacity for 10 million bits per second, written 10 Mb. Sometimes 56 Kb and 10 Mb are mistaken to mean, respectively, 56,000 and 10 million bytes per second. A byte is 8 bits, so actually a 56 Kb WAN can transmit 7000 bytes per second. The actual amount of application data that can be transmitted is decreased by the number of bits the transmission protocol uses to ensure accuracy of transmission. On a LAN, this can be up to 30 percent of the bandwidth. On a WAN 10 percent is reasonable.

client/server A protocol that has a rule that there can be only one exchange of messages between two programs. The first program, called the client, sends a message requesting a service to another program, called the server. The server can respond only once, presumably with the results of performing the service.

commit The process by which the effects of a transaction are made permanent. When a DBMS commits, it writes the updated information to disk in the permanent storage area.

conversational Conversational protocols set rules that allow two programs to send messages back and forth until one of them terminates the conversation. Between two programs, if the protocol allows either of them to initiate the conversation, the programs are said to be peers, and the protocol is called peer to peer. Some systems have a protocol that allows only one of the two programs to start the conversation; these systems provide conversational mode processing but not peer to peer.

daemon A process that is always running, waiting to detect a condition it must respond to and begin processing. Software servers and network listeners are daemons. The name dates back to the beginnings of UNIX when people were fond of anthropomorphizing the computer. The spelling is from Old English.

distributed database A database with its data spread over more than one platform, transparent to the application. *Distributed database* and *distributed processing* are vastly different and should not be confused.

distributed processing The processing of an application can proceed on more than one platform. A distributed processing application may use the various platforms in parallel or serially, depending on the application requirements. Sometimes the term *cooperative processing* is used to describe the distributed processing technique whereby the processes of the application communicate with each other and work together to complete a transaction.

found set The set of rows that are the result of an SQL SELECT. If the SELECT is against a single table, then all the rows are from that table. If the SELECT creates a join or other operation that results in a new table, the found set is the resulting table with the selection criteria applied.

kernel The central part of an operating system. This term is usually used only in reference to UNIX and means the non-removable part of UNIX.

listener In a network, a background process, always running, that detects that the network has information for the platform.

optimizer In this book, the component of a database management system that analyzes each access request, the nature of the data in the database, and the available indexes to determine the best method to examine the values in the database when executing the request. Optimizers are especially active during join operations.

paradigm A pattern, an example; in general usage, a way of doing things. In this book the way of doing things with the mainframe is contrasted with the way of doing things with open systems, especially UNIX.

peer-to-peer communications A protocol between two programs that allows either program to initiate a conversation and exchange messages.

prepare The term often applied to the first phase of two-phase commit. When a resource manager, such as a database responds with an okay vote, it is said to have completed the prepare phase. At this point, the database must be ready, or prepared, to roll back or commit any changes made by the transaction under any circumstances.

protocol A set of rules which must be followed to accomplish a desired result. In a client/server environment, there may be several protocols (the transmission protocol, the transaction management protocol, the client to server protocol, etc.). Systems enforce protocols by checking that the rules are followed and rejecting any request that does not follow the proper protocol. Usually an application program need not be aware of the protocols it is using. A notable example in which the application must be carefully programmed to follow the proper protocol is advanced peer-to-peer communications.

recovery In this book, the process of completing in-doubt transactions after a system failure. Transaction managers and DBMSs usually provide utilities for recovery, which are effective when used with two-phase commit.

remote procedure call (RPC) A method whereby a program can invoke a subroutine on another platform as if that subroutine were local. Ideally, a program should not be aware that it is using RPC, but many RPC systems require that the program perform certain actions and include special parameters in an RPC. There continues to be considerable discussion about how to implement RPCs in various environments. RPC usage by itself does not always ensure transaction integrity.

resource manager The component that manages a computer's shared resources. The resource manager has many responsibilities, including proper implementation of two-phase commit and managing the resource to ensure its integrity. In many systems, the DBMS is the only resource manager, but a resource manager may manage any resource, such as a money vending machine.

rollback See abort.

saturation The network capacity for carrying data is approached. Saturating a network may decrease the total data throughput of the network and in severe and prolonged cases may cause the network to become inoperative.

symmetrical multiprocessing (SMP) A method of managing multiple processors that allows any application to run on any processor. An SMP system will run efficiently without requiring special programming, though use of appropriate distributed processing systems will aid SMP in providing the best performance.

transaction Any group of processes that must complete, including updates to resources, in its entirety or leave no traces of ever having been attempted. A transaction is completed successfully by committing the transaction. A transaction may be aborted. A transaction has the ACID properties.

transaction integrity Work done during a transaction was done in accordance with transaction rules. If transaction integrity is lost, the user can no longer be certain that all updates are completed or all updates have been rolled back. In more technical terms, loss of transaction integrity means that the ACID properties have been lost.

transaction manager In its purest sense, that part of the system that maintains transaction integrity on a transaction. Many people refer to the entire transaction processing system as a transaction manager. Care must be used to understand the context in which this term is used.

transaction semantics Providing transaction management to processes. Most RPC systems do not include transaction semantics, which means they do not provide a transaction manager.

Bibliography

Allen, D. Dewey, "Distributed Computer Architectures for the 90s." *Oracle Integrator*, Volume 3, Number 6 (December 1992), 18–21.

Berson, Alex, *APPC: Introduction to LU6.2.* New York: McGraw-Hill, Inc., 1990.

Chorafas, Dimitris N., *Beyond LANS—Client/Server Computing.* New York: McGraw-Hill, Inc., 1994.

Dewire, Dawna Travis, *Application Development for Distributed Environments.* New York: McGraw-Hill, Inc., 1994.

Gagliardi, Gary, *Client/Server Computing.* Englewood Cliffs, NJ: PTR Prentice-Hall, 1994.

Gorman, Michael M., *Enterprise Databases in a Client/Server Environment.* New York: John Wiley & Sons, Inc., 1994.

Gray, Jim, and Andreas Reuter, *Transaction Processing: Concepts and Techniques.* San Mateo, CA: Morgan Kaufmann, 1993.

Kockan, Stephen G., and Patrick H. Wood, editors, *UNIX Networking.* Carmel, IN: Hayden Books, 1989.

Ozsu, M. Tamer, and Patrick Valduriez, *Principles of Distributed Database Systems.* Englewood Cliffs, NJ: Prentice-Hall, Inc., 1991.

Salemi, Joe, *Guide to Client/Server Databases.* Emeryville, CA: Ziff-Davis Press, 1993.

Schreiber, Richard, and William R. Ogden, *Distributed CICS,* New York, NY: John Wiley & Sons, Inc., 1994.

Shaw, Myril C., and Susan S. Shaw, *UNIX Internals.* Blue Ridge Summit, PA: TAB Books Inc., 1987.

Sobell, Mark G., *Practical Guide to UNIX System V*. Menlo Park, CA: Benjamin/Cummings Publishing Co., Inc., 1985.

Ullman, Jeffrey D., *Principles of Database and Knowledge-Base Systems, I & II*. Rockville, MD: Computer Science Press, Inc., 1988.

X/Open Company Limited, *Distributed Transaction Processing: XA Specification*. Reading, Burke, UK: X/Open Company Limited, 1992.

The following periodicals have been especially useful to the author:

COMPUTERWORLD, Box 9171, 375 Cochituate Road, Framingham, Mass. 01701-9171.

LAN TIMES, McGraw-Hill, Inc., 1221 Avenue of the Americas, New York, NY 10020.

Network Computing, CMP Publications Inc., 600 Community Drive, Manhasset, NY 11030-3875.

Open Systems Today, CMP Publications Inc., 600 Community Drive, Manhasset, NY 11030-3875.

Index

Access
  file, 11, 53
  frequency of, 40, 42
Access groups, 151
Access privileges, 148
Access to information, 22
Accidental access, 55
Administration functions, 167
Administration management, 104
Administration tools, 125–126
Administrative control, 55
Administrative services, 16
Advanced Program-to-Program Communications (APPC), 145
AIX, 144
Alias, 109
Application executables, 83
Application packages, 85
Application processes, 4
Application program, 98
Application program residence, 76

Application-specific security, 152
ASCII, 101
Asynchronous, 108
ATMs, 145
Atomical treatment of transactions, 163
Authentication, 101, 153–154
Authentication service, 153
Authenticator, 155
Authority, 59
Authorization, 154–156
Authorized personnel, 148
Automatic translation, 114
Average load, 74

Backup, 121
Backup copy, 121
Backup servers, 120
Bandwidth, 25, 33–34, 40, 52, 72, 73, 119
Banyon Vines, 36
Basic mapping service (BMS), 144